Law Essentials

SUCCESSION LAW

Law Essentials

SUCCESSION LAW

Frankie McCarthy, Ph.D.
Lecturer,
The School of Law,
University of Glasgow

DUNDEE UNIVERSITY PRESS
2013

Published in Great Britain in 2013 by
Dundee University Press
University of Dundee
Dundee DD1 4HN

www.dundee.ac.uk/dup

ISBN 978 1 84586 128 5

No natural forests were destroyed to make this product;
only farmed timber was used and replanted

British Library Cataloguing-in-Publication data
A catalogue for this book is available on request from the British Library.

Typeset by Waverley Typesetters, Warham
Printed by Bell & Bain Ltd, Glasgow

CONTENTS

TABLE OF CASES

TABLE OF STATUTES

A NOTE ON TERMINOLOGY

Adult relationships in Scotland may be legally formalised through marriage, for opposite-sex couples, or civil partnership, for same-sex couples. The law of succession does not distinguish between these different institutions. For the sake of brevity, reference to marriage or divorce within this book is accordingly intended to include registration and dissolution of civil partnership, and reference to a spouse is intended to include reference to a civil partner. Throughout the text, a surviving spouse will be referred to as female and her deceased partner as male, to reflect the statistical reality that most couples are made up of two members of the opposite sex, and that women tend to live longer than men. It is recognised, however, that in many situations the sexes may be reversed, or the parties may be of the same sex.

1 INTRODUCTION

Succession regulates what happens to a person's property when they die. It is one area of law which will almost certainly affect us all. Rules of succession are found in the earliest records of law in Scotland, and in many cases it is surprisingly easy to trace the current rules back to those in place as long ago as the 14th century. In general, the same principle has always underpinned the system: to distribute the deceased's property in the way he would have wanted. The law of succession usually aims to give effect to the deceased's wishes whether he made a will or not.

In most universities, succession is taught as a part of the property law course. However, in practice, succession questions frequently also involve family law, contract law and certain aspects of public law such as tax and citizenship rules. It is difficult for a practitioner in any area of private law to avoid succession entirely. A good grasp of the basics is essential, not least to deal with the inevitable questions from family and friends!

The key piece of legislation in this area is the Succession (Scotland) Act 1964, as amended, referred to in this text as the "1964 Act".

In recent years the Scottish Law Commission has published two reports recommending significant changes to the law of succession, the first (Scot Law Com No 124) in 1990 and the second (Scot Law Com No 215) in 2009. The Scottish Government indicated shortly after the publication of the 2009 Report that it intended to consult on the Commission proposals, but it does not appear that any progress has been made with this at the time of writing. The Commission's recommendations will be discussed throughout the book wherever relevant, although it should be kept in mind that the proposals may go through various changes before they are implemented, or may not be implemented at all.

PROPERTY: GENERAL RULES

The rules of succession deal with distribution of the deceased's estate. The estate comprises all property in the deceased's patrimony at the time of his death. A person's patrimony contains anything with a financial value that the person owns or to which he has some other legal right, such as a right to be repaid money that was lent to someone else.

A distinction is drawn in Scots law between heritable property and moveable property. The distinction is significant for succession since certain types of claim can be made over moveable property but not heritage and vice versa, the key example being legal rights (discussed in Chapter 4). Heritable property, also known as heritage or immoveable property, describes land and buildings. Anything which has become attached to heritage, such as trees in a garden, or a central heating system in a house, will also be regarded as heritage under the law of fixtures. Hereditary titles ("Marquis of Breadalbane") and coats of arms also fall within this category, although these are encountered infrequently in practice. A final, more complex, example is any right having "a tract of future time", meaning a right that can continue to be exercised on an ongoing basis into the future. A lease of a flat fits this definition, as does the right to payment of an annuity.

Moveable property covers everything which is not heritage, including corporeal moveable items – those with a tangible physical presence, such as a car or a table – and incorporeal moveable items such as money in a bank account or shares in a company. Personal rights, such as the right to payment of money arising under a contract, are also moveable property.

It is not usually difficult to determine into which of the two categories a given piece of property will fall, although more detailed discussion of the potential complexities can be found in K G C Reid, "Property", in *The Laws of Scotland: Stair Memorial Encyclopedia*, vol 18 (1993), paras 11–16.

Whether property is heritable or moveable will be determined as at the date and time of the deceased's death. In a limited number of cases, property can be converted from one category to the other for the purposes of distributing the estate. Imagine that the deceased was in the process of selling his house. At the time of death, he had agreed missives (the contract of sale) with the buyer, but had yet to transfer ownership or receive the purchase price in exchange. The house is therefore still in his patrimony, but legally must be transferred to the buyer. In these circumstances, the house would be considered as heritage with a value of zero, and the right against the buyer in respect of the purchase price as moveable property.

Conversion may also be constructive, where a testator has left instructions in his will that the executor should sell property in one category in order to acquire property in the other category for distribution.

Property will not form part of the estate where it involves *delectus personae*, meaning that it can be enjoyed only by the specific person by whom it was acquired. This arises in relation to certain types of leases, particularly residential leases, and may also be relevant in respect of contractual rights held against another person (such as in a contract of employment).

PERSONS: GENERAL RULES

Some basic rules govern who has capacity to inherit.

In the first place, it is not possible for a person to receive property from the estate unless they outlived the deceased. In other words, survivance is a condition of inheritance.

It is common for a person to make provision in his will for his children, and the law also provides children with certain default entitlements on the death of their parent. "Children" in this context are defined to include any person to whom the deceased was legally recognised as being a parent. It is not relevant that the child may have been born to parents who were not married. The concept of illegitimacy, which had historically been of considerable importance in the Scots law of succession, was abolished by s 21 of the Family Law (Scotland) Act 2006.

A child may be born subsequent to the death of his parent, described in law as a "posthumous child". In such a situation, a child *in utero* will be treated as already having been born for the purposes of succession. The child must survive birth before he is able to acquire ownership or any other legal rights in respect of inherited property, since a foetus has no legal capacity. The same assumption is not made in respect of a child posthumously *conceived* through assisted reproduction after the death of the man who would be legally recognised as his father, or the woman who would be legally recognised as his second female parent, under the Human Fertilisation and Embryology Act 2008. Sections 39, 40 and 46 of the 2008 Act allow the predeceasing parent to be registered on the child's birth certificate in this situation, but no rights in succession result. The parent could make provision for any posthumously conceived child in his or her will, however.

The position of adopted children is regulated by ss 23 and 24 of the 1964 Act, which provide that, for the purposes of succession, an adopted person is to be treated as the child of his adoptive parents and not of any other person. Accordingly, an adopted child will have no claim in succession against the estate of his biological parent, unless that parent has made specific provision for the child in his or her will. The Act contains a small number of exceptions to this rule, including in respect of persons adopted prior to the coming into force of the 1964 Act, but these are of increasingly limited significance in practice. Somewhat bizarrely, s 24(1A) provides that where the relative ages of siblings are important for rights of succession based on seniority, an adopted person is to be treated as if born on the date of the adoption order, although the Scottish Law Commission recommends in both the 1990 and 2009 Reports that this provision be repealed (para 7.34). The Commission also recommends that the provisions relating to the succession rights of adopted persons should be taken out of the 1964 Act and included more sensibly within the Adoption (Scotland) Act 1978 and the Adoption and Children (Scotland) Act 2007 (2009 Report, paras 7.29–7.35).

Step-children and those "accepted as a child of the family" in the terminology of the Family Law (Scotland) Act 1985 are not "children" for the purposes of succession. They have no claim on the estate of a *de facto* parent in the absence of any provision in the will. The exclusion of step-children and accepted children in this context is arguably out of line with their position in other areas of family law. However, the Scottish Law Commission considered that changing the succession rules would be likely to produce as many anomalies as it would resolve, and recommended that the position remain as it is (2009 Report, paras 2.31–2.34 and 3.43).

A surviving spouse or civil partner holds legal rights in respect of the estate of her late partner until divorce or dissolution. Mere separation, whether judicial or *de facto*, has no effect. Where provision has been made for a named spouse or civil partner in a testamentary writing, this provision is not affected by divorce or dissolution. For example, a legacy to "my civil partner, John Smith" will remain valid even if the partnership is dissolved. However, if the spouse or partner is not named, the legacy will go to whoever fulfils that description at the time of death. For example, a legacy to "my wife" will go to the woman married to the deceased at the time of his death. If he has no wife, the legacy will fall, as discussed in Chapter 7. Cohabiting partners have the ability to claim on their late partner's estate only if they were living together immediately prior to the death, following s 29 of the Family Law (Scotland) Act 2006, discussed in detail in Chapter 5.

Where the death in question is the result of murder, public policy dictates that the unlawful killer is an unworthy heir and accordingly forfeits any rights he may have held to succeed to his victim's estate. This is set out expressly in relation to a person who kills his parent or grandparent in the Parricide Act 1594, but common law makes clear that the rule is of more general application (*Smith, Petr* (1979)). The killer need not have been convicted in the criminal courts, however, a conviction creates a presumption of murder which any party challenging the verdict will be required to overcome on a balance of probabilities in subsequent civil succession proceedings. Although the law is not entirely clear, it seems that in such circumstances the estate will be distributed as though the unlawful killer had never existed, which might have a knock-on effect on the killer's children had they been in line to inherit: see the discussion of the rules of representation in Chapter 4. The Scottish Law Commission recommends that an unlawful killer who incurs forfeiture should be treated as having failed to survive the deceased (2009 Report, para 7.3). The forfeiture rule will not apply where the death has resulted from reckless driving (*Hardy* v *Motor Insurers' Bureau* (1964)) or where the killer is found not to have had the required *mens rea* for murder and is convicted instead of culpable homicide (*Re H (Deceased)* (1990)). The court also has power to attenuate the impact of the rule in the interests of justice under the Forfeiture Act 1982, provided that the killer has not been convicted of murder in the criminal courts.

DEBTS

The deceased's debts must be paid from the estate before any claims in succession can be satisfied. Certain debts are privileged, meaning that they must be paid before others. Deathbed and funeral expenses rank first. If they are paid in full, next in line are arrears of tax and social security, and payment of wages to employees for up to 4 months prior to the death. Once those are paid in full, all other creditors have an equal claim on the estate. If there are insufficient funds to cover all the debts, each creditor will receive an equal percentage of what they were owed by the deceased.

Creditors holding a right in security are in a different position from other creditors. They are able to obtain repayment by enforcing the security, usually by selling the property to which the right relates. Where the right in security is held over heritage (colloquially referred to as a "mortgage"), the debt which it secures will be considered a heritable debt, recorded in the inventory of the estate as a burden on the property to which the security relates. Heritable debts must be paid from the heritage in the estate. Moveable debts, which include all unsecured debts or debts secured on moveable property, must be paid from the moveables in the estate. If two securities exist in respect of the same debt, one held over heritage and one held over moveable property, the proportion secured over heritage should be paid from heritage, and the proportion secured over moveables paid from moveables.

Family members of the deceased may be able to claim financial support, known as aliment, from the estate. During lifetime, s 1 of the Family Law (Scotland) Act 1985 provides that a person must aliment his spouse, and also his children until they are 16 or until they are 25 if they are in full-time education or training. A person to whom this duty was owed immediately before the death can claim temporary aliment from the estate, to cover her financial needs during the period between the death and the distribution of the estate assets, if necessary. If the distribution of the estate does not leave her adequately provided for, she may also claim continuing support for as long as necessary from the beneficiaries of the estate, known as aliment *ex jure representationis*. Continuing support of this kind cannot be claimed by civil partners or accepted children, which seems to be an oversight in the law. Aliment is considered a debt on the estate, to be paid after the debts of ordinary creditors have been satisfied. Aliment claims of either type are extremely rare, since family members are usually provided for by legal rights (see Chapter 4). The Scottish Law Commission recommends that these claims should be abolished (2009 Report, paras 7.36–7.37).

As with that of a living person, the deceased's estate can be sequestrated (colloquially referred to as "going bankrupt") if the debts significantly exceed the assets. In such a situation, the expenses arising from the sequestration will be paid before any other debt, including funeral expenses. More information on the sequestration procedure can be found in F Davidson and L Macgregor, *Commercial Law in Scotland* (2nd edn, 2008), Chapter 8.

INHERITANCE TAX

When a person dies, the property in his estate becomes liable to inheritance tax (IHT). The rules on IHT are set out in the Inheritance Tax Act 1984, updated by various Finance Acts. (A Finance Act is passed every year to implement the changes set out by the Chancellor of the Exchequer in the Budget.) IHT is a large and complex subject which can be explored through the further reading listed at the end of this book. Certain aspects of succession law are difficult to grasp without a basic understanding of IHT, however, and so the main principles of the system are set out here.

Inheritance tax is charged on the total value of the property in the estate at the point of death, together with any property transferred out of the estate in the 7 years immediately preceding the death. This latter rule is to prevent people avoiding IHT by disposing of all their assets shortly before they die. All property in Scotland is subject to IHT, and all property outside Scotland owned by a person domiciled here is also liable.

Tax is charged at 0 per cent up to a threshold amount, set at £325,000 until April 2015. This means that where the total assets amount to less than £325,000, no tax is paid. Most intestate estates in Scotland fall within this limit. Any property exceeding the threshold is taxed at 40 per cent of its value. For example, imagine that the total assets are worth £400,000. The first £325,000 is charged at 0 per cent. The remaining £75,000 is charged at 40 per cent. The tax due will therefore be £30,000.

The IHT regime includes a number of exemptions. No tax has to be paid in respect of property transferred to the deceased's spouse on death or in the preceding 7 years. The same is true of property given to charities or certain other protected beneficiaries, such as political parties. Some types of property, usually of historical or cultural interest, are exempt where they are available for public access. Tax relief is also provided for certain types of business property and for transfers in quick succession, among other things.

It is common for people with a lot of assets to take advice on how to make the most of these exemptions in order to minimise the amount of inheritance tax to be paid on their death. This is referred to as "executry planning" or "executry tax planning". Succession cases are sometimes easier to understand in the knowledge that the provisions of a will or decisions taken by the parties involved may have been motivated by the tax consequences.

Responsibility for valuing the estate and ensuring that tax is paid rests with the executor, whose role is discussed in Chapter 2. Payment must usually be made within 6 months of the date of death. In practice, inheritance tax is always the first debt on the estate to be paid, since the executor will not be confirmed until this happens.

Current information on inheritance tax liability and exemptions can be found on the HM Revenue and Customs website at http://www.hmrc.gov. uk/inheritancetax/index.htm.

INTERNATIONAL PRIVATE LAW

Complications arise where the deceased is a Scottish person living in Scotland who owns property in another part of the world, or where the deceased is a person living elsewhere in the world who owns property in Scotland.

Where the deceased is Scottish, moveable property will always be dealt with under the Scots law of succession, regardless of where the property is to be found in the world. Heritage, however, will be dealt with by the *lex situs* – the law governing the place where the property is located.

Where the deceased is domiciled elsewhere, but has left property in Scotland, questions of succession are likely to be regulated by an agreement between the UK and the jurisdiction in question, although the type of property involved may also influence the outcome.

For a detailed account of the IPL rules, see E B Crawford and J M Carruthers, *International Private Law in Scotland* (2nd edn, 2006), Chapter 18.

Essential Facts

- The law of succession sets out the rules on what happens to a person's property after death.
- The deceased's estate is made up of all the property in that person's patrimony on death.

- Property can be heritable (land and buildings) or moveable (everything else). Certain succession rules will affect only heritable property, while others will affect only moveable property.
- A person must survive the deceased in order to inherit property from the deceased's estate.
- Children of the deceased will include adopted children, children born out of wedlock and children *in utero* at the time of the death. It will not include step-children, accepted children or posthumous children.
- If the deceased was murdered, his unlawful killer may not be entitled to inherit from the estate.
- Debts, including inheritance tax, are the first thing to be paid from the estate. If the deceased had more debts than assets, no-one will receive an inheritance.

2 EXECUTORS AND THE ADMINISTRATION OF THE ESTATE

The executor is the person responsible for ingathering the deceased's estate, paying his debts and distributing legacies to the beneficiaries. Any person aged 16 or over may act as an executor. The office is gratuitous, meaning that there is no entitlement to remuneration, unless it is specifically provided for in the will. It is common for two or more executors to act together, particularly in respect of a large estate.

An executor-nominate is a person nominated for the role by the deceased in the will. Where the deceased has not named anyone, or where the person nominated refuses or is unable to act, the Executors (Scotland) Act 1900 provides alternatives. In the unlikely event that the deceased has named some other trustee in the will, they will be deemed to have been nominated also as executor. A general disponee, universal legatee or residuary legatee (see the discussion in Chapter 7) will also be deemed to have been nominated. If more than one person fulfils these conditions, they can act jointly. Any person nominated either expressly or under the 1900 Act has the option to decline the office.

Where there is no executor-nominate, usually because there is no will, someone must petition the sheriff to be appointed in the role. An executor obtaining office through this process is known as an executor-dative. The law sets out an order of preference as to who is entitled to be appointed in the role. Top of the list is the surviving spouse if prior rights will exhaust the estate. Otherwise, relatives of the deceased are entitled to be appointed in the same order in which they are entitled to inherit under s 2 of the Succession (Scotland) Act 1964, discussed in detail in Chapter 5. If no executor can be found from these categories, next in line will be creditors of the deceased, then legatees, and finally the procurator fiscal or a judicial factor. If more than one person in a particular category seeks to take on the role, they will be appointed as joint executors. At present, the court cannot refuse to appoint a person as executor-dative unless another person in a preferred category is competing for the office. The Scottish Law Commission has recommended that the court have power to refuse the appointment of a petitioner who appears unsuited for the role (2009 Report, paras 7.13–7.16).

The first thing the executor must do is follow the procedure for obtaining confirmation to the estate. Confirmation is the court order which gives the executor legal title to deal with the deceased's assets. In order to apply for confirmation, the executor must prepare an inventory listing all the property in the deceased's estate, whether the property is within Scotland or elsewhere, and its value. The law does not specify the form in which the inventory must be prepared or the circumstances in which a professional valuation of property must be acquired as opposed to the executor's reasonable estimate. However, conventions tend to apply as a matter of legal practice. More detail can be found in MacDonald, *Succession*, paras 13.29–13.44. Once the inventory is prepared, the executor must swear an oath (or affirm, in keeping with religious beliefs or lack thereof) before a justice of the peace, sheriff court official or notary public that it is a "full and true inventory" of the contents of the deceased's estate.

Provisional inheritance tax will be calculated on the basis of the inventory. Where inheritance tax is due, this must be paid by the executor (who may need to obtain a loan to do so), with payment receipted on the inventory form by HM Revenue and Customs.

The executor can then apply to the sheriff clerk for confirmation, lodging the inventory along with his application. An executor-nominate must also lodge a copy of the will naming him as executor. At present, the court cannot refuse to confirm an executor-nominate, but the Scottish Law Commission has recommended that such a discretion be introduced where the proposed executor is unsuited to the office, in line with its proposals on appointment of an executor-dative (2009 Report, paras 7.13–7.16).

An executor-dative, in addition to the inventory, is required to lodge a bond of caution (pronounced "kayshun"), which is a financial guarantee that he will make the estate furthcoming – in other words, that he will distribute the assets to the beneficiaries. Caution is usually provided in the form of an insurance policy, meaning that if the executor does embezzle from the estate, the beneficiaries will receive compensation from the insurer. It is not necessary for caution to be lodged where the executor is the surviving spouse inheriting the entire estate in prior rights, following s 5 of the Law Reform (Miscellaneous Provisions) (Scotland) Act 1985. The Scottish Law Commission has argued that the requirement to find caution places a disproportionate financial and administrative burden on the executor and recommends that it should be abolished (2009 Report, paras 7.6–7.12).

The certificate of confirmation is the executor's proof to other parties that he has legal title to deal with the estate assets. If the executor subsequently discovers assets which were not included within the inventory for confirmation, he must produce a corrected inventory, and will then be granted an "eik" to his confirmation which includes the newly discovered property. Where an executor deals with assets without confirmation, this is known as "vitious intromission" with the estate, and may result in the executor becoming personally liable for any debts.

Once the certificate of confirmation has been issued, the executor can begin ingathering the deceased's assets and satisfying his debts. He has an obligation to pay any debts of which he becomes aware, so long as there are funds to do so. Creditors, unless they hold a right in security, must make their claims within 6 months of the death in order to receive a percentage should the estate turn out to be insolvent. Creditors' claims made after the 6-month period should be paid if there are remaining funds. The practical effect of these rules is that the executor cannot start distributing legacies to the beneficiaries until after the 6-month period has passed, unless he is very sure that there are no debts outstanding. If he distributes the estate only to find that a claim is subsequently made by a creditor, he may become personally liable for that debt.

When debts are paid, the executor then distributes the estate to the beneficiaries under the will or following the rules of intestate succession. At the stage of the final distribution, after payment of any outstanding inheritance tax, the beneficiaries are entitled to see a full account of the executor's dealings. At this point, the executor should seek a discharge from the beneficiaries, by which they acknowledge that they have received their due and there can be no further challenge to the executor's intromissions with the estate. This will not prevent a beneficiary from making a claim for breach of trust if it is subsequently discovered that the executor has acted outwith his powers, however.

It is not necessary to obtain confirmation to a small estate, following the Confirmation to Small Estates (Scotland) Act 1979. A small estate is currently defined as one where the gross value does not exceed £36,000 prior to deduction of debts and funeral expenses. The value is increased from time to time by statutory instrument to take account of inflation. In the case of a small estate, a simplified procedure is available, where the sheriff clerk assists an uncontested executor to complete the inventory and the other formalities. However, a bond of caution is still needed.

EXECUTOR AS TRUSTEE

The executor of an estate is also a trustee. A trust is a legal concept in which one person, called the trustee, owns property which he is only allowed to use for the benefit of someone else, or for specific categories of people, known as beneficiaries. The easiest way to understand the concept of a trust in Scotland is to imagine that the trustee has two patrimonies. The first is his personal patrimony, containing all his assets and liabilities, which he can use or dispose of as he pleases. The second is the trust patrimony, containing trust assets and liabilities, which can only be used for the beneficiaries. The truster is the person who put the property into the trust patrimony in the first place, and who gave instructions on who the beneficiaries should be and how the property should be used by the trustee to benefit them.

In the context of succession, the truster is the deceased. The trustee is the executor, and the content of the trust patrimony is the property in the estate. The executor-trustee may only administer the property for the good of the beneficiaries, namely the deceased's heirs under the will or under the rules of intestacy.

Since the executor is a trustee, the general law of trusts applies to his dealings with the estate. The powers and responsibilities of trustees are principally contained in the Trusts (Scotland) Act 1921 and the Trusts (Scotland) Act 1961. In particular, the trustee is in a fiduciary relationship with the beneficiaries, with the result that he must take reasonable care in how he deals with the trust property, and he will be liable to the beneficiaries if he does not live up to that standard. Since the trust property is held in a separate patrimony, any difficulties affecting the trustee's personal patrimony – for example, if he goes bankrupt – have no effect on the trust property. Detailed information on the law of trusts can be found in G L Gretton and A J M Steven, *Property, Trusts and Succession* (2009), Chapters 22, 23 and 24.

Essential Facts

- The executor is the person responsible for gathering in and then distributing the deceased's estate.
- The deceased may name an executor in the will. This is known as an executor-nominate.
- If there is no executor-nominate, usually because there is no will, an executor-dative is appointed to the role. An executor-dative is usually the deceased's closest living relative.
- The executor prepares an inventory of the estate, then seeks a court order called confirmation, based on the inventory. Confirmation gives the executor legal title to deal with the property.
- The executor pays the deceased's debts, and distributes all remaining property in the estate to the beneficiaries.
- The executor is a trustee in respect of the contents of the estate.

3 DEATH AND SURVIVORSHIP

The starting point for operation of the law of succession is a person's death. Usually, determining whether a person is dead or alive is a straightforward question of medical fact. Complications may arise, however, where a person is "brain dead" or being kept alive by machines. The Registration of Births, Deaths and Marriages (Scotland) Act 1965 provides that a physician must issue a certificate of death specifying the cause of death (s 24), which must be registered within 8 days of death or of discovering the body (s 23). If the circumstances of the death are unusual or suspicious, the procurator fiscal will conduct enquiries which may lead to a post mortem or a public inquiry.

No-one has a right of ownership over the body of the deceased, which is in the custody of the executor until disposal by burial, cremation or any other lawful method. It is not clear who has the right to decide on what should happen to the body. The deceased may have expressed a preference in the will or in some other way, but there is no obligation on the executor or next-of-kin to adhere to this, nor is there authority as to whose wishes should prevail in a dispute between executor and next-of-kin. Burials are regulated by the Burial Grounds (Scotland) Act 1855. Cremations, which must be applied for after the death, are governed by the Cremation Acts 1902 and 1952, and the Cremation (Scotland) Regulations 1935. The local authority has responsibility to arrange for disposal of the body if no-one else has done so (s 50(1) and (6) of the National Assistance Act 1948). Any person making payment for funeral expenses has a right of relief against the deceased's estate, paid first before other expenses from the estate.

Where a person is missing but their body has not been found, the Presumption of Death (Scotland) Act 1977 will apply. The Act provides that an application to the court for declarator of death may be made in respect of a person who is thought to have died, with declarator to be granted where death is proved on a balance of probabilities. This test is likely to be satisfied where, for example, a boat has sunk far from land and no survivors can be found: a person who was on the boat is more likely to be dead than alive. In this situation, s 2 provides that the court will fix the date of death as being the last day on which the person might, as a matter of proof, have been thought to be alive. Alternatively, an application for declarator may be made after 7 years in respect of a person who has not been known to be alive throughout that period of time. This would be relevant, for example, where a healthy person has simply disappeared and no evidence is available to suggest that he has died rather than simply moving elsewhere to begin a new life. In this situation, s 2 provides that the date of death will be the day occurring 7 years after the person was last known to be alive.

Declarator has the same effect as a certificate of death. The rules of succession begin to operate. If the missing person was married or in a civil partnership, that relationship is dissolved, and will not revive should it later transpire that the missing person is actually still alive. Declarator does not, however, absolve the missing person of responsibility for any criminal offence committed while they were believed to be dead, as set out in s 3 of the 1977 Act.

Declarator can be varied (changed) if further evidence becomes available as to the circumstances of the death, or recalled if the missing person is subsequently found alive. This will not have any effect on rights to the missing person's property acquired by other people as a result of the declarator, unless the court thinks it is fair and reasonable to make an order varying these rights. An application for an order varying property rights must be made within 5 years of the date of declarator. Under ss 5–6 of the 1977 Act, the executor has a duty to take out insurance when distributing an estate on the basis of a declarator, in case this situation arises.

SURVIVORSHIP

The order in which people die can be significant in the law of succession, since a dead person cannot inherit. Imagine that Anna and Bert are friends, each of whom has made a will leaving their entire estate to the other. If Anna dies first, Bert will inherit her estate. On Bert's death, his whole estate, including the possessions he has inherited from Anna, will go to someone else. However, if Bert dies first, Anna will inherit his estate, with the property going elsewhere on Anna's death.

Usually, there will be no difficulty in establishing who died first. However, situations can arise in which several people are killed by the same event, such as a car crash. This is referred to as a "common calamity". In such a situation, it may not be possible to ascertain the order of death as a matter of fact. To allow for the rules of succession to operate, the Succession (Scotland) Act 1964 sets out presumptions as to the order of death in situations where proof is not possible.

The general rule provided in s 31 is that a younger person will be presumed to have survived the elder. There are two exceptions. In the first place, this presumption does not apply as between spouses or civil partners, who will instead be presumed to have died simultaneously regardless of their ages, replicating the common law prior to the 1964 Act (*Ross's JF* v *Martin* (1955)). The second exception arises where the elder person has made provision for the younger person in his will, and specified an alternative beneficiary to take the place of the younger person should they die before the elder person (known as a "destination over"). In that situation, if the younger person has not made a will, the usual presumption will be reversed, meaning that it will be presumed that the elder person has survived the younger.

As an example, imagine that Carol's will states that her car should go to her grandson, David, unless he dies before Carol does, in which case the car should go to her friend Ellen instead. Carol and David both die in the same accident. It is impossible to ascertain the order of their deaths. If David has made a will, the usual presumption will apply. David, as the younger party, will be presumed to have survived Carol and will inherit the car, which will then be distributed along with the rest of his estate in terms of his will. If David has not made a will, applying the usual presumption would have the undesirable result that the car falls into his estate, only to be distributed under the rules governing intestacy. This is not an attractive outcome, since the intestacy rules are only a default, deemed to represent what the deceased would have wanted. It would be better to respect the express direction given by Carol as to who should inherit the car, rather than relying on the "best guess" of the intestacy regime. Accordingly, the exception operates: Carol will be presumed to have survived David. The car will accordingly be inherited by Ellen.

The Scottish Law Commission recommended in its 1990 Report that s 31 be replaced by a more straightforward provision to the effect that, in a common calamity where the order of deaths is unknown, the estate of each party who died should be distributed as though the other(s) had failed to survive them. In other words, the rule which currently applies to spouses should apply across the board in a common calamity. This recommendation was repeated in the 2009 Report at paras 6.55–6.57.

Essential Facts

- Once a certificate of death is issued in respect of a person, the rules of succession will begin to operate.
- The Presumption of Death (Scotland) Act 1977 allows for a declarator of death to be issued where no body can be found. Declarator triggers the succession rules in the same way as a death certificate.

- Declarator will be issued straight away where it is more likely that a person is dead than alive. If there is no evidence either way, declarator will be issued after a person has been missing for 7 years.
- For succession purposes, the law presumes that a younger person will have survived an elder person where they both died in a common calamity.
- This presumption does not apply (a) to spouses, or (b) where the elder person had made a will providing an alternative beneficiary to the younger person, and the younger person was intestate.

4 LEGAL RIGHTS

The surviving spouse or civil partner and any child of a deceased person have an indefeasible entitlement to inherit a share of the estate. This entitlement, known somewhat confusingly as "legal rights", arises automatically on the deceased's death, and can be claimed regardless of whether the estate is testate or intestate. In other words, it is not possible for the deceased to disinherit his spouse or children. Legal rights have been recognised in the common law of Scotland since before records began, with the entitlement of a surviving spouse recently extended to a surviving civil partner by s 131 of the Civil Partnership Act 2004. Significant reforms proposed to the legal rights regime by the Scottish Law Commission will be discussed at the end of the chapter.

ENTITLEMENT

Legal rights can be claimed only over the moveable property in the estate. One consequence of this is that a person might effectively defeat a legal rights claim by arranging before death for his entire estate to be made up of heritage.

A surviving spouse is known in law as the relict. The legal rights entitlement of the relict is known as *jus relicti* (for a widower) or *jus relictae* (for a widow). For a surviving civil partner, reference is usually made simply to rights under s 131 of the Civil Partnership Act 2004. In this chapter, references to *jus relictae* include references to *jus relicti* and to rights under s 131.

The relict is entitled to one-half of the deceased's moveable estate if the deceased has not left behind any children, or to one-third of the moveable estate if there are children. The relict must have survived the deceased, and remained married to him at the point of death, or no legal rights entitlement will arise. Imagine that Eve dies, leaving behind moveable estate of £9,000. If she has no children, her husband Fred will be entitled to half of the moveable estate (amounting to £4,500). If she has children, Fred will be entitled to one-third of the moveable estate (amounting to £3,000).

The legal rights of children of the deceased are known as legitim. The legitim fund is made up of one-half of the moveable estate if the deceased has not left behind a spouse, or one-third of the moveable estate if there is a spouse. If there is more than one child, the legitim fund will be shared equally between them, known as *per capita* division. Imagine that George dies, leaving behind moveable estate of £9,000. If he has no spouse, the legitim fund will be £4,500. His three children, Hilary, Ian and Jack, will each receive an equal share of the fund, being £1,500 each. If George is survived by a spouse as well as the children, the legitim fund will be £3,000. This will again be divided equally among the children, with each receiving £1,000.

Section 11 of the 1964 Act provides for representation in legitim. This means that, where a child predeceases his parent, his entitlement to legitim is passed down to his own children (the deceased's grandchildren). Representation is infinite, meaning that if the grandchildren have also died before the deceased, great-grandchildren can inherit in their place, and so on through the generations. Where representation operates, the grandchildren will be entitled to claim only what their parent would have received from the estate. Where legitim is distributed between descendants of different degrees of relationship to the deceased in this way, it is known as *per stirpes* division of the legitim fund. Look again at the example above of George, who has died leaving £9,000 of moveable estate. He is not survived by a spouse. The youngest of his three children, Jack, died before him, leaving behind twin daughters, Jennifer and Jill. As before, the legitim fund will be £4,500. As before, Hilary and Ian will each receive £1,500 as their share of the fund. The remaining £1,500, which would have gone to Jack, will be shared by his daughters, who will each receive £750 accordingly.

COLLATION

The law assumes that a parent intends to treat each of his children equally. Accordingly, if the parent during his lifetime gives a gift to one child but not to their siblings, it is assumed that the gift is an advance payment of the child's legitim. The advance must therefore be taken into account when legitim is distributed following the parent's death. The is known as collation *inter liberos*

The collation principle has its basis in common law, and has been expressly preserved by s 11(3) of the 1964 Act. For collation to operate, in the first place a collatable advance must have been received by one (or more) of the legitim claimants. Regular payments made in the discharge of parental duties, such as paying for food, clothing or school fees, will not meet this test. What is required is a gift that goes beyond the norm. Hiram gives the examples of setting a child up in business, or furnishing his home (para 3.10). A gift of heritage cannot be collatable: legitim cannot be claimed from heritable property, and so a gift of heritage cannot be seen as an advance payment of legitim. A loan given by a parent to his child should be distinguished from a collatable advance, since the child will be under an express obligation to repay this money to the estate as part of the original agreement with the parent: the doctrine of collation is not required in order to make the money liable to repayment.

Collation operates by notionally adding the value of the advance to the existing legitim fund. The overall fund is split between the legitim claimants following the usual rules. The child who has received the advance then takes his share of the legitim fund minus the amount he has already received in the form of the advance.

As an example, the siblings Hilary, Ian and Jack above were each entitled to an equal share in the legitim fund of £4,500, meaning that they received £1,500 each. Now, imagine that Hilary had received a collatable advance of £600 from her father during his lifetime. This advance must be considered part of the legitim fund, increasing the fund's value from £4,500 to £5,100. This should be split equally between the three children, entitling them to £1,700 each. Ian and Jack will each receive £1,700. Hilary has already received £600 of her £1,700 share in legitim, so she will receive a payment of £1,100. Each of the children has therefore received £1,700 in legitim. Ian and Jack received the full amount on their father's death. Hilary received £600 during her father's lifetime and the remaining £1,100 on his death.

In the example above, the advance paid to Hilary was less than her eventual entitlement to legitim. Had the advance exceeded her legitim entitlement, she may have been required to pay money back into the legitim fund at the time of her father's death.

It should be noted that collation does not operate automatically, but has two caveats. In the first place, the child who has received the advance must be called on to collate by his siblings. This may not happen if, for example, the siblings were not aware that the advance was paid by the parent during his lifetime. Second, a child who does not claim legal rights cannot be made to collate. Accordingly, a child who has received significant advances of legitim during the lifetime of his parent would be advised to renounce any claim to legal rights if he wishes to maximise his financial reward from the estate.

EXTINGUISHING LEGAL RIGHTS

Legal rights can be extinguished through satisfaction, discharge or prescription.

Satisfaction

Legal rights will be satisfied where their value is paid to the claimant by the executor of the estate. Once payment has been received, it is not possible for the claimant to change his mind and discharge his rights.

Discharge

Legal rights can be discharged (renounced) by the claimant. If the discharge is effected prior to the death of the deceased, the estate including any other legal rights claims will be distributed as though the discharging claimant had never existed (*Hog* v *Hog* (1791)). This is because rights discharged prior to the deceased's death have not yet vested in the claimant. (Vesting is discussed in Chapter 10.) For example, where a widow discharges her claim to *jus relictae* prior to the death of her husband, on his death the legitim fund will be made up of one-half of the moveable estate, as though he had left behind only children. In the legal terminology, the widow's share accresces to the legitim fund.

However, if (as is more commonly the case) the discharge does not take place until after the deceased has died, this has no effect on the legal rights entitlement of other parties. This is because the rights have vested in the beneficiary at the point of the deceased's death (*Fisher* v *Dixon* (1840)). If the widow above does not discharge her claim to *jus relictae* until after her husband's death, the legitim fund will remain as one-third of the moveable estate notwithstanding the discharge. Similarly, if a child discharges his entitlement to legitim after the death of his parent, his share of the fund does not go to other siblings. In other words, accretion does not operate. The value of the discharged legal rights will instead be made available to satisfy legacies if the deceased was testate, or will fall into the free estate if the deceased was intestate.

The Scottish Law Commission has recommended, at para 2.54 of its 2009 Report, that the distinction between discharge prior to death and discharge after death be removed. In each case, it recommends that the estate should be distributed as though the claimant who has discharged their rights did not survive the deceased.

Legal rights are most commonly discharged where alternative provision has been made for the claimant in the deceased's will. In such a situation, the claimant cannot take both his inheritance under the will and his legal rights entitlement. He must elect to take one or the other. This requirement is referred to as the doctrine of "approbate and reprobate". Hiram explains that "to claim both is a contradiction, since it would be simultaneously to accept and reject the same instrument", namely the will. The claimant must receive proper legal advice on the consequences of making an election, or else the election may not be valid (*Dawson's Trustees* v *Dawson* (1896)). A provisional election may be made before full advice is received, in which case the claimant retains the right to revoke the election, as demonstrated in *Harvie's Executors* v *Harvie's Trustees* (1981). There is no time limit during which the election needs to be made, unless there is a good reason why another legal rights claimant requires the decision to be taken within a particular time frame. Should the claimant accept his inheritance under the will, his legal rights claim will be considered to have been discharged implicitly. In practice, an executor is likely to require the claimant to execute a formal document of discharge, not least because only an express discharge will bar any claim which might otherwise arise should an estate subsequently fall into intestacy or partial intestacy (*Nasmith* v *Boyes* (1899)).

Prescription

If a claim to legal rights is neither satisfied nor discharged, it will be extinguished through the law of prescription 20 years from the date of death, following the Prescription and Limitation (Scotland) Act 1973, ss 6 and 7.

DEFEATING LEGAL RIGHTS

Although it is not possible to exclude legal rights claims in a will or by any other mechanism, it is possible for a person to arrange his affairs in such a way that a claim will not have any value. As noted above, an estate made up entirely of heritage will mean that there is no property from which legal rights can be claimed. More drastically, a person might arrange to have no property in his patrimony at all on his death. Although both techniques would be effective in defeating legal rights, it is obvious that both present significant challenges in reality, not least because it is rare that a person will know the date of his death in advance. The only foolproof way to avoid legal rights claims is to remain unmarried and have no children!

REFORM

In Chapter 3 of its 2009 Report, the Scottish Law Commission recommended substantial reform to the law of legal rights. It considered the current law to be flawed in various respects. In particular, the fact that legal rights can be claimed only from the moveable estate was argued to be somewhat arbitrary, as well as making it possible for such claims to be defeated by the deceased arranging for his estate to be made up entirely of heritage on his death. Additionally, the rigid nature of legal rights did not allow any account to be taken of the needs and resources of claimants, which could lead to unfair results particularly where legitim is claimed by adult children. The appropriateness of protection from disinheritance in present-day Scottish society was called into question, although the Commission accepted that public opinion evidence maintained a level of support for these rules to remain in place.

The Commission recommended abolition of legal rights, to be replaced by "legal shares". These new claims, held, as before, by surviving spouses and children, would be exigible over the whole of the estate, rather than restricted to moveable property. Legal shares could be claimed regardless of whether the estate was testate or intestate, although, as under the current law, a party entitled both to a legal share and to provision under the will would be required to elect which to take. Any party entitled to claim a legal share would be able to renounce that claim with no effect on the entitlement of any other legal share claimant, regardless of whether the renunciation occurred before or after the death.

The legal share of a surviving spouse would equate to 25 per cent of what she would have been entitled to take had the deceased died intestate. The current provisions on intestacy, and the changes proposed to these rules by the Commission, are discussed in Chapter 5.

In relation to the legal share of children of the deceased, two alternatives were suggested. The simpler option is that children would be entitled to 25 per cent of the sum they would have received had the deceased died intestate. This claim would be exigible against the whole estate and would be shared among the children on a *per capita* basis, with representation to apply as it currently does in respect of legitim claims. The doctrine of collation would no longer apply.

The second, more controversial, option is that legitim would be abolished and not replaced. Instead, a dependent child would have the right to claim a capital sum from the estate representing the amount required to maintain him until he is no longer dependent. Children would be defined as dependent where the deceased owed them an obligation of aliment (financial support) under the Family Law (Scotland) Act 1985, meaning those aged under 16, or under 25 in full-time education or training. The value of the sum would be assessed by reference to various criteria, including the needs, resources and earning capacity of the child, the financial circumstances of any other person owing an obligation of aliment to the child and whether the beneficiary of the estate from which the child's entitlement would be taken is the child's other parent. This latter option is preferred by the Commission, although it has been subject to significant criticism, which can be explored through the further reading listed at the end of this book.

Essential Facts

- The surviving spouse or civil partner and any children of the deceased are always entitled to claim legal rights over the moveable estate, whether the deceased has left a will or not.
- The spouse is entitled to a third of the moveable estate if the deceased has also left behind children, or half of the moveable estate if there are no children.
- Children of the deceased are entitled to a third of the moveable estate shared equally among them if there is a surviving spouse, or half of the moveable estate shared equally among them if there is no spouse.
- Grandchildren may claim legal rights in place of their predeceasing parent. This is known as representation.
- Where a parent gives a gift to one child but not to any of that child's siblings during the parent's lifetime, the law presumes that this was intended to be an advance payment from the child's inheritance. The gift will therefore be taken into account in calculating the value of legal rights claims under the doctrine of collation.
- Legal rights may be extinguished through satisfaction, discharge or prescription.
- The Scottish Law Commission has recommended that legal rights be replaced by "legal shares": for a spouse, 25 per cent of what she would have received on intestacy; for a child, either 25 per cent of what they would have received on intestacy, or a capital sum based on their needs for dependent children only.

Essential Cases

Coats' Trustees v Coats (1914): Archibald Coats died, leaving behind two sons and three daughters. All of the children had received collatable advances from their father during his lifetime. All of the children had also been provided for in his will. One daughter, Evelyn, elected to take legitim rather than her inheritance under the will. The question was whether Evelyn and/or her siblings required to collate in this situation. The court noted that the doctrine of collation was an equitable doctrine designed to preserve equality among siblings when the legitim fund was divided. In this case, since only one child was concerned with the distribution of the legitim fund, there was no place for collation to operate. All the advances were accordingly ignored in calculation of the legitim claim.

Dawson's Trustees v Dawson (1896): Mrs Dawson elected to take her inheritance under her late husband's will rather than her entitlement to *jus relictae*, based on legal advice she had received as to the value of the two different claims. It subsequently became clear that the legal advice had been wrong. The widow wished to revoke her election. The court found that, since there had been an error, and since nothing had happened as a result of her election which could not be undone without too much difficulty, she was free to revoke her election and take her legal rights entitlement instead.

Harvie's Executors v Harvie's Trustees (1981): Mrs Harvie had to choose between provision under her husband's will and her legal rights entitlement. After advice from a lawyer, she continued to live on her husband's farm, which was considered to be a provisional election in favour of the will, since she would have had no right to the farm in *jus relictae*. While she awaited a statement from the accountant on which to base her final election, she died. The court was satisfied that her actions were enough to amount to an election. It also indicated that, since the election was not injurious to her pecuniary interests, the election was binding despite the fact that she had not received full legal advice.

5 INTESTATE SUCCESSION

Where a person dies without making a will or any other provision for what should happen to his property on death, he is described as intestate. The law sets out a series of rules as to how an intestate estate should be distributed. The rationale underlying the rules is that they should, so far as possible, replicate what the deceased would have wanted to happen. The rules are primarily set out in the Succession (Scotland) Act 1964. The Scottish Law Commission has recently recommended significant reform in this area, discussed at the end of the chapter.

WHEN IS A PERSON INTESTATE?

A person is intestate when he dies leaving all or any part of his estate "undisposed of by testamentary disposition", according to s 36(1) of the 1964 Act. The meaning of "testamentary disposition" is discussed in Chapter 6, however the most common example is a will. Property disposed of on death by a mechanism other than a testamentary disposition – the most frequent example will be a survivorship destination in the titles of a house, discussed in Chapter 9 – does not form part of the intestate estate.

The deceased may have left a will covering only certain items within his estate. This is known as partial intestacy. The rules of intestate succession will be applied in full to the part of the estate which is not covered by the will.

ORDER OF DISTRIBUTION

The first payments from any intestate estate are debts owed by the deceased. Prior rights are then paid to a surviving spouse or civil partner. Legal rights will then be paid out of any remaining moveable estate to a surviving spouse and/or any children of the deceased. Finally, the free estate will be distributed.

Where the deceased was in a cohabiting relationship on death, any claim by the cohabitant under s 29 of the Family Law (Scotland) Act 2006 (discussed below) will be paid after debts, prior rights and legal rights of the surviving spouse (if there is one), but *before* payment of legitim.

PRIOR RIGHTS

The surviving spouse or civil partner of an intestate is entitled to claim prior rights under ss 8 and 9 of the 1964 Act, as extended to civil partners by s 10(2) of the Civil Partnership Act 2004. It may help to think of prior rights as a mechanism by which to ensure the surviving spouse continues to have a home and be financially stable following the death of her partner, preventing her from becoming a burden on the state.

Prior rights entitle the surviving spouse to three things: a dwellinghouse; furnishings for that house; and a lump sum of money. These rights can only be paid if there are sufficient assets in the estate with which to pay them. For example, if the deceased did not own a dwellinghouse on death, it is not possible for the spouse's claim in that regard to be satisfied. Each of the rights can be claimed independently of the others, however.

The financial value of each of these claims is altered by the government from time to time, to take into account inflation and changes in the value of property, among other things. The current financial limits, which will be discussed below, were set by the Prior Rights of Surviving Spouse and Civil Partner (Scotland) Order 2011 (SSI 2011/436) and have been in force since 1 February 2012.

The housing right

The first entitlement of the surviving spouse is to the interest of the deceased in a dwellinghouse. Under this right, the spouse will usually be expected to inherit the deceased's share in the family home, whether the deceased was the sole owner of the property, or shared ownership of the home with the spouse or another party.

"Dwellinghouse" is defined in s 8(6) of the 1964 Act. The definition is very wide, including houses and flats along with more uncommon types of home such as caravans and houseboats. A garden or other ground attached to the home is also included.

In order for prior rights entitlement to arise, s 8(1) provides that the deceased must have had a "relevant interest" in the property, usually meaning ownership or a share in ownership. A tenant's interest in the property will also be "relevant", although the Act sets out various restrictions to inheritance of certain forms of tenancy under this right.

The surviving spouse must have been ordinarily resident in the dwellinghouse at the time of the deceased's death, as defined in s 8(4). What is meant by "ordinarily resident" will depend on the type of dwellinghouse in question. Ordinary residence in a holiday home in the countryside might only entail residence every few weekends, for example. However, a house in the deceased's estate in which the spouse has never resided – for example, a flat bought as an investment and rented out to others – will not be available to satisfy payment of the housing right.

Where the deceased had a relevant interest in more than one house in which the surviving spouse was ordinarily resident, the spouse must elect which of the properties she wishes to inherit under the housing right. Provision is made for this in s 8(1), which states that an "election" must be made within 6 months of the date of death.

The entitlement of the surviving spouse under this head is capped at a value of £473,000. Since the purpose of the provision is to prevent the surviving spouse from becoming homeless, rather than to maximise her claim over the intestate estate, the entitlement is to a share in a house and not to property up to a value of £473,000. This means that if, for example, the deceased had a relevant interest in a family home worth £250,000 and also a holiday cottage worth £100,000, with the surviving spouse ordinarily resident in both, the spouse must still elect which of these two properties is to be taken under the housing right. The spouse cannot claim both simply because the combined financial value falls under the limit of £473,000.

If the deceased's relevant interest in a property exceeds the statutory financial limit, the spouse will instead be entitled to a capital sum payment of £473,000. The spouse may also receive a capital sum if the property had been used by the deceased "for carrying on a trade, profession or occupation", if the value of the estate as a whole is likely to be diminished by distributing the house separately from the rest of the business. This might arise, for example, if the property in question is a farm house and the surviving spouse would not inherit the rest of the farm business. If the deceased held a relevant interest in a tenancy which cannot be transferred rather than a share of ownership, the spouse will again receive a capital sum payment rather than transfer of the interest itself in satisfaction of her entitlement under the housing right.

The furniture right

As a complement to the housing right, the surviving spouse is also entitled to "furniture and plenishings" under s 8(3) of the 1964 Act. "Furniture and plenishings" are defined by s 8(6)(b) to cover most common household items including domestic animals, but excluding cash and securities along with any goods used for business purposes. Heirlooms are also excluded. The current financial limit on this entitlement is £29,000.

The spouse is only entitled to claim furniture from a house in which she was ordinarily resident prior to the deceased's death. As with the housing right, where the spouse was ordinarily resident in more than one home, she must elect from which home she wishes to inherit the furniture within 6 months of the date of death, under s 8(1). It is not necessary for the surviving spouse to elect the same home in respect of the furniture right as she elected in respect of the housing right, although this would generally be expected to happen as a matter of common sense. It might also be noted that s 25 of the Family Law (Scotland) Act 1985 sets out a presumption that spouses and civil partners share ownership of household goods within the family home. Accordingly, where the surviving spouse takes furniture from the family home in satisfaction of her prior rights entitlement here, it should be recalled that the deceased owned only a half-share in the household goods: the other half-share is already in the ownership of the surviving spouse.

The money right

The final prior rights entitlement of the surviving spouse is to a sum of money, as set out in s 9 of the 1964 Act. The amount varies depending on whether the deceased has also left behind issue (children, grandchildren and further descendants): the surviving spouse is entitled to take £89,000 if there are no issue, or £50,000 otherwise.

The statute provides that the money right should be paid "out of the parts of the intestate estate consisting of heritable and moveable property respectively in proportion to the respective amounts of those parts". This means that the percentage of the money right to be paid from the heritable property should be equivalent to the percentage of the remaining estate which is made up of heritable property. Similarly, the percentage of the money right to be paid from the moveable property should be equivalent to the percentage of the remaining estate which is made up of moveable property.

This is best illustrated with an example. Assume that, after the housing and furniture rights have been satisfied, there is £200,000 remaining in an intestate estate. £150,000, or 75 per cent of the estate, is made up of heritage; £50,000, or 25 per cent of the estate, is made up of moveables. The deceased has left behind both a spouse and issue, so the spouse is entitled to £50,000 in satisfaction of the money right. Of the remaining estate, 75 per cent is made up of heritage, so 75 per cent of the £50,000, or £37,500, should be paid from the heritage; 25 per cent is made up of moveables, so 25 per cent of the £50,000, or £12,500, should be paid from the moveables. The surviving spouse will accordingly receive £37,500 of heritage and £12,500 of moveables. Added together, this amounts to the £50,000 to which the spouse is entitled in terms of the money right.

If, after distribution of the housing right and the furniture right, the estate amounts to less than the spouse is entitled to in terms of the money right, the entitlement will be satisfied by transfer to the surviving spouse of the entire remaining estate.

In a partially intestate estate, the value of any legacy to which the surviving spouse is entitled under a testamentary deed must be offset against the money right, following s 9(6)(b). The meaning given to this provision by s 36(1) is wide enough to include a share in property received by the spouse by virtue of a survivorship destination, or the proceeds of a life insurance policy in respect of the deceased. However, any legacy to which the spouse would have been entitled anyway in terms of the housing right or the furniture right need not be offset against the money right.

For example, Kevin dies intestate. His estate comprises a half-share in the family home worth £150,000, and savings of £25,000. His share in the home is subject to a survivorship destination in favour of his civil partner, Luke. Luke will receive Kevin's share in the house by virtue of the survivorship destination. If the survivorship destination had not existed, Luke would have received the half-share in the house anyway by virtue of the housing right. Accordingly, it is not necessary for Luke to offset the value of Kevin's share in the house against his entitlement to the money right. Luke will therefore inherit Kevin's entire estate, with Kevin's half-share in the family home transferred to Luke via the survivorship destination, and the savings of £25,000 transferred to Luke in satisfaction of the money right. (Luke's entitlement to the housing and furniture rights will simply fall away, as there is nothing in the estate with which these rights can be paid in this example.)

Where a spouse has been left a legacy which *would* have to be offset against the money right, she may elect to take the money right in full and renounce her claim to the legacy.

LEGAL RIGHTS

Following payment of prior rights, the remaining moveable estate is then subject to legal rights claims by the surviving spouse and any issue of the deceased. Legal rights are explained in Chapter 4.

INTESTATE SUCCESSION

All property, whether heritable or moveable, remaining in the estate following satisfaction of legal rights claims is referred to as the "free estate". It is also sometimes known as the "dead's part" in recognition of the fact that this is the only part of the estate over which a deceased would have had full freedom to test. The 1964 Act, somewhat confusingly, refers to the free estate as the "intestate estate". In order to avoid confusion, that terminology will not be used here.

Section 2 of the 1964 Act sets out a hierarchy of categories of people related to the deceased. The closest relative to the deceased based on this hierarchy is known as the next-of-kin. Where any surviving relatives exist in the top category, the entire free estate will be shared among them. If there are no survivors in this category, inheritance will fall to relatives in the second category, and so on through the categories. As with legal rights, the doctrine of representation operates to enable children to share the entitlement of their predeceasing parent within each of the categories.

At the top of the hierarchy of relatives are descendants of the deceased. Surviving children will share the entire free estate on a *per capita* basis. If a child has died before the deceased leaving behind grandchildren, the estate will be divided on a *per stirpes* basis. (For an explanation of the meaning of "*per capita*" and "*per stirpes*", see Chapter 4.) As discussed in Chapter 1, the definition of "children" includes posthumous children and adopted children but not step-children of the deceased.

If there are no surviving descendants, inheritance will pass to the next category of relatives, described as parents and "collaterals" (siblings), which includes adoptive parents and siblings. Half of the estate will pass to the surviving parent or parents and the other half to the surviving sibling or siblings, to be shared equally among them. If only parents(s) or only sibling(s) survive the deceased, they are entitled to the entire free estate. Representation operates in respect of siblings, with division of the estate on a *per stirpes* basis where a predeceasing sibling is survived by issue. Half-blood siblings are entitled to inherit only if no full-blood siblings of the deceased survive, although the Commission recommended in its 2009 Report that this distinction should be removed (para 2.37). Neither step-parents nor step-siblings are entitled to inherit.

If the deceased is not survived by descendants, parents or siblings (including nieces and nephews), the inheritance will fall to the surviving spouse or civil partner. The hierarchy then goes on to include more distant relatives: aunts and uncles, grandparents, siblings of grandparents and any more remote relations. Finally, if no surviving relative can be found, s 7 of the 1964 Act provides that the Crown is entitled to the free estate as *ultimus haeres* (the "final heir"). This function is exercised on behalf of the Crown by the Queen's and Lord Treasurer's Remembrancer, who will accept applications for claims on the estate from persons who may be considered to have a moral right to inherit.

COHABITANTS

Following the introduction of the Family Law (Scotland) Act 2006, a person who lived in a cohabiting relationship with the deceased at the time of death may make a claim on the intestate estate. "Cohabitant" is defined in s 25 of the Act as either member of a couple consisting of a man and woman who were living together as if husband and wife, or two persons of the same sex living together as if civil partners. To determine whether this definition has been met in a particular case, the court is directed to consider the length of time during which the parties lived together, the nature of their relationship during that period and the nature of any financial arrangements between them during that period.

The right of a cohabitant to claim on intestacy is set out at s 29(1). The court is empowered to make an order for a capital sum or a transfer of property to the surviving cohabitant after consideration of the factors listed in s 29(3). These are: the size and nature of the net intestate estate; any benefit received or to be received by the survivor in consequence of the deceased's death from somewhere other than the intestate estate (for example, death in service benefit or the proceeds of a life insurance policy); the nature and extent of any other rights against or claims on the deceased's net intestate estate and any other matter the court considers appropriate. The only specific guidance the court is given as to the level of any award is that it must not exceed what a surviving spouse is or would have been entitled to receive under the 1964 Act regime.

From the wording of the legislation, it is difficult to ascertain what a cohabitant might expect to receive from an application under s 29. The Scottish Law Commission notes that the award does not seem intended to achieve any particular aim, such as ensuring the financial stability of the cohabitant, or providing her with what the deceased would have wanted her to receive. In the second case decided under these provisions, *Windram, Applicant* (2009), Sheriff Janys M Scott, QC indicated that it was unclear whether fairness in this context implied placing the cohabitant in the position a surviving spouse would have been in, or protecting the rights of surviving children to what they would have been entitled to under the 1964 Act regime.

The two cases decided under the provisions to date provide limited guidance. In *Savage v Purches* (2009), the sheriff was satisfied that the surviving cohabitant had lived with the deceased as though they were civil partners, but did not believe any award to be justified. In part, this was because the applicant was already in receipt of a substantial sum (relative to the size of the estate) as the proceeds of life insurance. Additionally, the deceased had not made a will specifying the applicant as a beneficiary, although evidence demonstrated that the deceased *had* done so in respect of an earlier long-term cohabiting partner. (The will had been destroyed when that earlier relationship came to an end.) In *Windram, Applicant*, the applicant was found to have been living with the deceased, as though married, for over 20 years, during which the couple had raised two children and operated a successful fish and chip shop business together. With the aim of striking a balance between the rights of the applicant and those of the children, the sheriff awarded the applicant £11,000 less than she would have been entitled to as a surviving spouse: enough to repay the outstanding loan on the family home which was held entirely in the name of the deceased.

Further case law is likely to follow. However, case law may not be able to answer the fundamental question of what the award to a cohabitant is designed to achieve. Changes to the legislation may be required.

PROPOSALS FOR REFORM

The Scottish Law Commission has recommended significant reform to the rules of intestate succession, contained within Chapter 2 of its 2009 Report. It notes that intestate estates are most commonly those of lower value; wealthier parties are more likely to make a will. The law of intestacy should accordingly focus on achieving the most equitable resolution for modest estates. In the Commission's view, the current rules produce very different results based on factors which are somewhat arbitrary, such as the proportions of the estate made up of heritage and moveable property, and how much of the estate property falls within the categories covered by prior rights. The Commission's aims in recommending the reforms are to simplify the law, and to recognise a surviving spouse as one of the deceased's main heirs, with the particular goal of ensuring that she does not have to leave the matrimonial home as a result of the death.

To simplify the law, the Commission first recommends that where the intestate is survived by a spouse but no children, the whole of the net intestate estate should be inherited by the spouse. The current law, by which the deceased's parents and/or siblings would be entitled to a share in this situation, was considered out of step with modern societal conceptions of family. Where the deceased is survived by issue but no spouse, the issue should share the entire net intestate estate, as under the current law.

Where the deceased is survived by both spouse and issue, the Commission recommends that the current prior rights regime be replaced by a simpler system where the spouse is entitled to a fixed amount from the estate, known as the "threshold sum". There would be no stipulations as to which property in the estate should be taken in satisfaction of the threshold sum. The Commission tentatively suggests a figure of £300,000 as appropriate, although it recognises that this is really a question of political judgement for the government should the recommendations be implemented. Any property remaining in the estate after payment of the threshold sum should be split between the surviving spouse and the issue.

After consideration, the Commission did not recommend that the surviving spouse should have a legal right to purchase the family home. The legislative regime required "would be disproportionate to the mischief that it would be designed to address" given that, in the huge majority of cases, the threshold sum would take up the entire estate anyway. It does recommend, however, that where the deceased's share in the home passes to the spouse under a survivorship destination (discussed in Chapter 9), the value of that share should be deducted from the spouse's threshold sum entitlement. Where the value of the deceased's share in the family home exceeds the threshold sum, the excess amount should be deducted from the net intestate estate and the remainder of the estate split between the spouse and the issue, ensuring that the spouse would remain in the home.

Step-families created some complications for the Commission. In the first place, it was recognised that the general policy by which the spouse takes the majority of the estate may not be considered fair where the spouse is not the mother of the deceased's children, typically because she is his second wife. The potential unfairness here may be illustrated by an example. Imagine that Mark dies intestate, leaving behind his wife Nadia and two children. His estate is less than the threshold sum. Nadia will take the whole estate and his children will inherit nothing. Nadia dies 2 years later. Her estate comprises whatever is left of her inheritance from Mark as well as her other property. If she is the mother of Mark's children, it is likely they will inherit the bulk of her estate, meaning that effectively the property of both parents has ultimately been handed on to their children. If she is not the mother of Mark's children, this will not happen, since step-children have no automatic claim on the estate of step-parents. The estate may be inherited by Nadia's children from a previous relationship. Mark's children will never receive anything from his estate. This is the result that the Commission identified as potentially unfair in terms of societal expectations of inheritance.

Despite recognising the difficulty, the Commission did not believe that the complex statutory regime that would be needed to obtain different results would be justified. A party in this situation should, instead, make a will protecting his children.

On a related note, the Commission considered whether step-children and children accepted as members of the family should have a claim on intestacy against step-parents and *de facto* parents. Financial claims based on these relationships are increasingly found in other areas of family law. Again, although it was accepted that unfairness might result from excluding such children in all situations, complex statutory provision was considered to be disproportionate to the problem. It was recommended that step-children and accepted children continue to be excluded from the intestacy regime.

Finally, the Commission recommends that where a person renounces any entitlement to inherit from the deceased's estate, the estate should accordingly be distributed as though that person had not survived the deceased, regardless of whether the renunciation takes place before or after the deceased has died. Such a person should also be able to renounce any claim by their issue that might result from this renunciation, which is not possible under the current law.

The Commission also recommends radical reform to the rights of a cohabiting partner on intestacy. The recommendations are set out in Chapter 4 of its 2009 Report. It suggests that the ambiguity which affects s 29 of the 2006 Act cannot be resolved by case law, given the lack of guidance available to the court in the legislation. Instead, it recommends that the section be repealed and a new regime introduced. Under the new scheme, the court would first be required to determine whether the claimant and the deceased had been cohabiting in the legal sense. This should be established through reference to a non-exhaustive list of criteria, considering whether they were members of the same household; the stability of the relationship; whether they had a sexual relationship; whether they raised children together; and whether they appeared to other people to be a married couple, civil partners or cohabitants.

If the applicant met the legal definition of "cohabitant", the entitlement of a surviving spouse in the same circumstances as the cohabitant should be calculated under the law of intestate succession. The cohabitant would then be entitled to a percentage of the amount a surviving spouse would have received, with the percentage determined on the basis of the share the cohabitant has "earned" during the course of the relationship. The three factors to be taken into account in determining this percentage are: the length of the period of cohabitation; the interdependence (financial or otherwise) between the applicant and the deceased; and the contributions (financial or otherwise) of the applicant to their shared life. The Commission suggests that where the couple had been together for many years and raised a family, the award would be 100 per cent of what a surviving spouse would have received. For a young couple together for only 5 years with no children and separate finances, 25 per cent might be more appropriate.

The Commission suggests that cohabitants should be free to renounce their rights on intestacy whether before or after the death, and also sets out special rules to apply in the case where an intestate is survived by both a spouse and a cohabitant.

Essential Facts

- An estate is intestate where the deceased did not leave a will.
- Where an estate is intestate, prior rights are paid first, followed by legal rights. Anything remaining is known as "free estate".
- Prior rights can be claimed by the surviving spouse or civil partner, and comprise a share in a house (up to a value of £473,000), furniture (up to a value of £29,000) and a lump sum of money (£50,000 if the deceased left behind children, £89,000 if not) to be taken "rateably" (proportionately) from the heritage and moveables in the estate.
- Legal rights of the spouse and/or children, as discussed in Chapter 4, are then paid from the remaining moveable estate.
- Finally, any free estate remaining is distributed to the deceased's nearest relative(s) as determined by the hierarchy set out in s 2 of the 1964 Act.
- A surviving cohabitant of the deceased may make a claim under s 29 of the Family Law (Scotland) Act 2006. At present, there is little guidance on how much a cohabitant might expect to receive.
- The Scottish Law Commission has recommended substantial reform to the rules of intestate succession. A spouse should inherit the whole estate if there are no children. The children should inherit the whole estate if there is no spouse. Where there is both a spouse and children, the spouse should receive a threshold sum (a suggested figure of £300,000) and the remainder should be split between the spouse and children.

Essential Cases

Savage v Purches (2009): Graham Voysey died leaving no will. Savage was his cohabiting partner and made a claim on his estate under s 29 of the 2006 Act. The defender was the deceased's half-sister, who stood to inherit the whole estate under the law of intestacy. In determining the claim, the court was satisfied that the pursuer and the deceased had "lived together" within the meaning of the Act, but did not make an award to the pursuer. Savage had already received a sizeable inheritance, relative to the size of the estate, as the proceeds of a life insurance policy in respect of the deceased. Additionally, Savage and Voysey did not have a shared bank account and Voysey had not made a will naming Savage as a beneficiary, all of which suggested to the court that the deceased would have intended Ms Purches to inherit rather than Mr Savage.

Windram, Applicant (2009): William Giopazzi died leaving no will. Windram was his cohabiting partner and made a claim on his estate under s 29 of the 2006 Act. The action was defended by a *curator ad litem* representing the interests of the couple's children, who stood to inherit the whole estate under the law of intestacy. The court was satisfied that the couple had "lived together" within the meaning of the Act for around 25 years. They had raised two children and run a business together, although all assets were in the deceased's name. The court accepted that Ms Windram was essentially in the same position as a spouse, and made an award close to what a surviving spouse would have received on intestacy, with a small deduction to take account of an additional sum Ms Windram had received under an insurance policy. The court hoped that this approach would balance the rights of Ms Windram with those of the children.

EXAMPLE INTESTACY CALCULATION

In this example, the rules on legal rights and intestacy outlined in Chapters 4 and 5 are used to demonstrate how an intestate estate would be distributed among the various claimants.

James dies in an accident. He has not left a will. He leaves behind a wife, Lily, two sons, Harry and Ron, and two granddaughters, Ginny and Luna. The grandchildren are the children of his daughter, Hermione, who died last year.

On death, James's estate comprises:

- a one-half share in the family home, which he had bought together with Lily. The house is worth £450,000 in total;
- furniture worth £20,000. This includes a set of antique table and chairs passed down to James by his grandfather, which are worth £5,000;
- a holiday cottage on Skye worth £50,000;
- furniture for the holiday cottage worth £7,500;
- investments worth £25,000;

- his stamp collection, valued at £10,000;
- a motorbike worth £12,500;
- savings of £40,000.

	Heritable	Moveable	Total Estate
House share	£225,000		£225,000
Furniture		£15,000	£15,000
Antiques		£5,000	£5,000
Holiday cottage	£50,000		£50,000
Cottage furniture		£7,500	£7,500
Investments		£25,000	£25,000
Stamp collection		£10,000	£10,000
Motorbike		£12,500	£12,500
Savings		£40,000	£40,000
TOTAL	**£275,000**	**£115,000**	**£390,000**

Prior rights

Section 8(1): housing[1]	£225,000		
Section 8(3): furniture[2]		£15,000	
	£50,000	£100,000	£150,000
Section 9: money[3]			
Heritage: 50 × 50 / 150	£16,666		
Moveables: 50 × 100 / 150		£33,334	
Subtotal	**£33,334**	**£66,666**	**£100,000**

---

[1] Lily will have to elect which of the two houses to receive, assuming she was ordinarily resident in both prior to James's death. I have assumed she will elect to take the more valuable family home. She is entitled to a share in a house up to a value of £473,000.

[2] Again, Lily will have to elect which furniture she wishes to take, and I have again assumed she has gone for the most valuable. The antique table and chairs will be excluded from the definition of "furniture" by s 8(3) of the Succession (Scotland) Act 1964. Lily is entitled to furniture up to a value of £29,000.

[3] Lily and James have children; accordingly, Lily is entitled to claim £50,000.

Legal rights[4]

Jus relictae (66,666/3)	£22,222
Legitim (66,666/3)	£22,222[5]

Intestate Estate	**£33,334**	**£22,222**	**£55,556.00**

Harry	£18,518.66
Ron	£18,518.66
(Hermione)[6]	£18,518.66

Division of the legitim fund

Total fund: £22.222

Children: 3

Each child receives: £22,222/3 = £7,407.33

Hermione's share will be split between her two children, so Ginny and Luna will receive £3,703.66 each.

Summary of division of estate

Lily

Housing right	£225,000
Furniture	£15,000
Section 9 money	£50,000
Jus relictae	£22,222
TOTAL	**£312, 222**

Harry and Ron

Legitim	£7,407.33
Free estate	£18,518.66
TOTAL	**£25,925.99 (each)**

---

[4] As James has left behind a wife and children, Lily will be entitled to one-third of the remaining moveables as *jus relictae*. The children will be entitled to one-third of the remaining moveables as *legitim* to be shared equally among them.

[5] This amount, known as the legitim fund, will be split between the remaining children.

[6] Since Hermione predeceased her father, her share will be split between her two children, who will therefore receive £6,172.88 each.

Ginny and Luna

Legitim	£3,703.66
Free estate	£9,259.33

TOTAL   **£12,962.99 (each)**

Final summary

Lily	£312,222.00
Harry	£25,925.99
Ron	£25,925.99
Ginny	£12,962.99
Luna	£12,962.99

TOTAL   **£389,999.96**

6 VALIDITY OF TESTAMENTARY WRITINGS

A testamentary writing is any deed which has testamentary effect. The most common example is a will. Valid creation of a testamentary writing requires both *essential validity* and *formal validity*. To be essentially valid, a will must have been created by a testator with both *capacity* and *intention* to test. To be formally valid, the will must meet the *statutory requirements* imposed on all legal writing, principally contained within the Requirements of Writing (Scotland) Act 1995.

A will is the most common form of testamentary writing. A will may often be one single document, but wills can also be made up of several documents, perhaps written and executed at different times. An addition to a will is known as a codicil. In general, a will operates to transmit the deceased's property into the hands of an executor, who then transfers it to the beneficiaries named in the will. A trust disposition and settlement is a more complex form of testamentary writing, transferring property on the testator's death into the hands of trustees who will administer property on behalf of the beneficiaries named in the deed.

INTENTION TO TEST

The testamentary writing must make it clear that the granter intended it to have testamentary effect. Hiram states: "The decisive factor is whether or not it can be established that the testator meant the deed in question to represent his or her concluded testamentary intention" (para 5.4). In other words, the document must represent the testator's final word on the matter of where his assets are to go on his death. A document indicating an intention to make a will at a later stage or sketching out some thoughts on what a person might wish to happen on their death will not meet this requirement. A letter to a solicitor instructing him to draft a will for the testator cannot represent a completed testamentary intention (*Munro v Coutts* (1813)).

CAPACITY

The testator must have had legal capacity to form a completed testamentary intention. There are two aspects to this. The testator must have passed the initial test of legal capacity, being of age and mentally capable. The testator's capacity must also have been exercised freely and not overcome by the will of another through facility and circumvention or undue influence.

In Scotland, a person has testamentary capacity from the age of 12 onwards, following s 2(2) of the Age of Legal Capacity (Scotland) Act 1991. Beyond that, the testator must have had sufficient mental capacity to understand the nature and consequences of his completed testamentary intention. There is no formal legal test in Scotland, but approval has been given (for example, in *Sivewright* v *Sivewright's Trustees* (1920)) to the classic English formulation set out in *Banks* v *Goodfellow* (1869–70):

> "It is essential to the exercise of such a power that a testator shall understand the nature of the act and its effects; shall understand the extent of the property of which he is disposing; shall be able to comprehend and appreciate the claims to which he ought to give effect; and, with a view to the latter object, that no disorder of the mind shall poison his affections, pervert his sense of right, and prevent the exercise of his natural faculties – that no insane delusion shall influence his will in disposing of his property and bring about a disposal of it which if the mind had been sound would not have been made."

Shortly put, the test requires that the testator understands the effect of his actions. It is not necessary that his intention be considered objectively fair or morally justifiable, only that it was made in full understanding of the results. For example, in *Morrison* v *MacLean's Trustees* (1862), the deceased left part of his estate for the benefit of his housekeeper, and the rest in trust for the education of boys named MacLean. No provision was made for any surviving family members. The court did not consider this in itself evidence of lack of capacity on the testator's part.

Capacity may not be a permanent state but may come and go in testators affected by conditions such as dementia and clinical depression. What is important is that the testator had the relevant capacity at the time when the will was executed. The court will not be quick to find that a testator lacked capacity as a result of mental illness. In *Ballantyne* v *Evans* (1886), the testator was seriously depressed and later committed suicide, but the court did not view this as sufficient to impact on his capacity to test. In *Smith* v *Smith's Trustees* (1972), the testator believed that his late wife had returned to him after her death, but the court did not consider this to have had any impact on the rationality of his will. *Nisbet's Trustees* v *Nisbet* (1871) confirms, however, that where the deceased was known to have suffered from a mental illness, the onus is on a person seeking to rely on the will to prove that it had been executed at a time when the testator was lucid. This is a reversal of the usual situation. It seems that where the terms of the will itself are irrational – for example, if the estate was left to the Man on the Moon – then the testator is likely to be found to lack capacity.

The testator may also have lacked capacity if under the influence of alcohol or drugs. The English decision of *Sharp* v *Adam* (2006) concerned a testator who had been suffering from multiple sclerosis. Evidence suggested that his mood was altered by the drug therapy he was receiving at the time of executing his will to such an extent that he was not rational. The will he had made at this time, which excluded his daughters entirely, was held to be invalid, and a previous will leaving everything to them was accordingly revived.

FACILITY AND CIRCUMVENTION

Where the testator did have capacity to test, the will may be subject to challenge on the basis that his intentions were not freely expressed. A will is invalid if it resulted from the illegitimate influence of a third party over the testator. In other words, if the testator wrote the will he did as a result of being put under pressure of one type or another, the will cannot stand.

The two most common challenges of this type arise from the related doctrines of facility and circumvention and undue influence. It is difficult to draw a clear boundary line between the two. Lord President Clyde gave a summary in *Ross* v *Gosselin's Executors* (1926):

> "The essence of undue influence is that a person, who has assumed or undertaken a position of quasi-fiduciary responsibility in relation to the affairs of another, allows his own self-interest to deflect the advice or guidance he gives, in his own favour. On the other hand, the essence of circumvention and facility is that a person practises on the debility of another whose individuality is impaired by infirmity or age, and moulds the inclination of the latter to his own profit."

In practice, it is possible if not common for both facility and circumvention and undue influence to have been present in the same case. A challenge to the validity of a will can be made on both grounds in the same application to court.

To establish the existence of facility and circumvention, three elements must be present: facility; circumvention; and lesion. The start point will be lesion, or loss. In the context of a will, this can be understood as loss suffered by the testator in the sense that his will did not express his freely formed intention, or loss suffered by a beneficiary who would have inherited had the testator's true intention been reflected in the will. As a matter of common sense, without a disappointed beneficiary, a challenge to the validity of the will is unlikely to be made.

Facility is defined by Hiram as "weakness of mind such that the mind of the person affected is easily swayed by that of another" (para 6.8). Although the case law does not set out a hard and fast test, the key concept is that the testator must have been more susceptible to influence or less able to resist suggestion than the average person. The level of suggestibility cannot be such that the testator lacks capacity entirely, however. Facility may have resulted from dementia, mental illness, drugs or alcohol, although the existence of any of these things does not automatically lead to the result that the testator was facile. It will be a question of fact in every case.

Circumvention is defined in *Bell's Dictionary* as "deceit or fraud", and described by Hiram as "pressure of some kind exerted on the testator by a third party" (para 6.09). This element of a challenge will often be difficult to evidence: the actions of a third party amounting to circumvention are unlikely to have been witnessed by anyone other than the testator and, by the time a challenge is brought, the testator is most likely to be dead. The court has been willing to infer the existence of circumvention where the degree of facility is high, loss is established and there is evidence of factual circumstances in which circumvention could have taken place.

The leading case of *MacGilvary v Gilmartin* (1986) is an example. The defender in this case was the pursuer's daughter. In the weeks immediately following the death of Mrs MacGilvary's husband, her daughter took her to a solicitor and had Mrs MacGilvary sign over her house to her daughter. Afterwards, the pursuer argued that she had been in a state of extreme grief at the time, such as to amount to facility, and had not known what she was signing. There was no specific evidence of circumvention on the daughter's part. The court found that the degree of facility and the level of lesion, together with the absence of any reasonable explanation of the daughter's behaviour, were sufficient to give rise to an inference of circumvention from the facts. The contract was accordingly set aside. More recently, in *Horne v Whyte* (2005), the testator had been heavily dependent on his housekeeper who had latterly looked after his legal affairs as well as his house and his health. Late in life, he made a codicil to his, will reducing the legacies to his family members in order to leave a substantial sum to the housekeeper. The court found that only circumvention on the housekeeper's part could have caused the amendments to the will.

UNDUE INFLUENCE

The closely connected doctrine of undue influence also has three constitutive elements: a relationship of trust between the testator and another party; an abuse of that trust; and an advantage obtained by the dominant party as a result. There does not need to be general facility on the testator's part for a challenge of this type to be successful. Instead, it is the nature of the trust placed by the testator in the dominant party that has enabled advantage to be taken by that person.

A relationship of trust will be likely to exist between the testator and a party with whom they are close personally or professionally. Such a relationship will be presumed between the testator and near relatives, as with the mother and son in *Gray* v *Binny* (1879). The relationship between a solicitor and a client was found to meet the test in *Ross* v *Gosselin's Executors* (1926). The relationship between the testator and her art dealer in *Honeyman's Executors* v *Sharp* (1978) also satisfied the test, although the evidence made clear that the art dealer had become close with the testator and was advising her on business affairs more generally by the time the will under challenge was executed. Relationships which fall within this category will generally be fiduciary or quasi-fiduciary, and their existence in each case will be determined as a matter of fact.

Evidence must also be brought of how that trust has been abused, perhaps through misrepresentation by the dominant party as to the effect of the will, or the actions of intended beneficiaries. It is important to demonstrate that the testator would not have listened to the dominant party, or taken heed of their actions, if it were not for the existing relationship of trust between the two. A testator would ignore a stranger on the street who suggested that his child did not deserve to inherit anything in his will, but the same testator may well act on this suggestion if made by a trusted adviser who claimed to be concerned for the testator's interests.

The dominant party must have received a benefit as a result of exerting influence on the testator. This would usually take the form of a legacy in the will that the dominant party would not otherwise have received, or a more generous legacy than might have been expected.

Given the nature of the undue influence doctrine, it should not be surprising that it is difficult to mount a successful challenge on this ground where the testator has received independent legal advice in relation to the will. This point was emphasised in *Gray* v *Binny* (1879).

Where facility and circumvention or undue influence are shown to have been present, the will can be reduced (set aside). If the testator had executed an earlier will, it may revive at this point, as outlined below, and the estate will be distributed according to its terms. This may be the situation most likely to result in a challenge of this type – it makes sense to imagine the children, say, to whom the entire estate had been left in the earlier will challenging the document executed by the deceased 3 days before his death leaving everything to his housekeeper. If no prior will exists, the estate will fall into intestacy and be distributed based on the default rules.

FORMAL VALIDITY

In addition to meeting the tests of essential validity, a will must also follow the rules for formal validity. The concern of the law here is with the document itself, which is subject to certain statutory requirements. The sample will at the end of Chapter 7 of this book gives an example of how a formally valid testamentary writing could look in practice. It should be noted that the rules in this area changed significantly on 1 August 1995. Documents executed prior to that date are subject to a different regime, explained in detail in Hiram, paras 5.5–5.12.

The current rules for formal validity are found in the Requirements of Writing (Scotland) Act 1995. The Act does not set out a particular form of document or set of words to be used, but gives some more general requirements. In the first place, the will must be in writing (s 1(2)(c)). A verbal statement cannot be a valid testament. The document must be subscribed by the granter, meaning that the testator must sign at the end of the last page of the will (s 2). Section 7 of the Act sets out three forms of signature acceptable in this context: the "longstop" method, where the testator signs using the full form of his name as employed in the will, such as "James Andrew Smith"; the "standard" method, where the testator signs using a full or abbreviated version of his forename together with his surname, such as "Jim Smith"; or the "informal" method, where the testator signs using any other name, description, initial or mark, such as "JAS" or "Dad".

Provided that the will is written down and has been subscribed by the testator, it will be formally valid.

If the will is to be implemented, however, formal validity will not be enough. The will must also be *probative*. The term "probative" means "self-proving". This is relevant where a challenge is made to the validity of a will. As a general rule, where a person seeks to rely on a deed, it is his responsibility to prove the validity of that deed. So, where a beneficiary seeks to rely on a will in order to claim a legacy, and another person challenges the validity of that will, the onus would be on the beneficiary to prove that the will had been validly executed. If the will has been made probative, however, the responsibility changes sides. Where a probative will is challenged, it is presumed that the will has been validly executed at the date and place narrated in the deed. The onus accordingly falls on the challenger to show that the execution was in some way defective. Given that the testator will often be dead by the time any challenge is brought to a will, making it difficult for evidence to be brought as to the circumstances in which the will was executed, it is particularly desirable for a testator to ensure that his will is probative so that his wishes will be respected after his death. On a more practical note, only a probative will can form the basis of confirmation of an executor-nominate.

To make a will probative, in the first place either the "longstop" or "standard" methods of signature must have been employed. It is not possible to make a valid will probative where it has been signed using the "informal" method ("Dad"). Two further steps must then to be taken for probativity. First, s 3(2) provides that the will must be signed by the testator on every page. In practice, the testator will usually subscribe on every page, although the Act requires only a signature on every page other than the last one. Secondly, s 3(1)(a) provides that the testator's subscription must have been witnessed.

The witnessing or attestation process is regulated by s 3. The witness must be 16 years of age or above, have full legal capacity and "know" the granter in the sense of being certain of his identity. The Act does not bar a beneficiary under the will from acting as a witness but, as a matter of good practice, this should not happen. The testator must subscribe the will in the presence of the witness, or acknowledge to the witness that the subscription is his signature. The witness then signs to confirm that the subscription is the testator's signature. This must be "one continuous process", meaning that the witness must sign immediately after watching the testator subscribe, or having the testator acknowledge his signature. The name and address of the witness must be added to the document after the witness has signed. This is usually contained in the "testing clause" which follows the end of the document. In signing, the witness confirms only that the subscription on the will is the testator's signature. The witness is not confirming the content of the will beyond that.

While the testator remains alive, it is always possible to convert a valid will into a probative will by virtue of the testator acknowledging his signature to a witness. After the testator has died, this will obviously no longer be possible. However, the Act allows for the will to be declared probative by the court following an application by any interested party under s 4. An executor-nominate may make an application under this section when seeking confirmation.

Alterations made to the will subsequent to subscription are not part of the document, unless the alteration itself is signed by the testator. In practice the testator will usually initial any changes for this reason. However, s 5 provides that alterations will be presumed to have been made prior to subscription in certain circumstances, including where the will is probative. Accordingly, the onus in most cases will be on a person arguing that the alteration was made after subscription to prove that this was the case as a matter of evidence.

In its 1990 Report, at paras 4.21–4.28, the Scottish Law Commission recommended that where a will prepared by a third party, such as a solicitor, failed to express the intentions of the testator correctly, a process should be available whereby an interested party could apply to the court to have the will rectified. The court should be expressly empowered to consult extrinsic evidence when determining whether the case for rectification has been made. This recommendation was reiterated in the 2009 Report at paras 6.1–6.7.

REVOKING A WILL

A testator may revoke his will at any point during his lifetime, provided that he has capacity and intention to do so. The capacity required to revoke a will is the same as that required to execute a will in the first place. The testator must not be rendered *incapax* through illness, injury or intoxication. Where the testator has both capacity and intention to revoke, he will nevertheless be unable to do so if he has contracted not to do so with a beneficiary. The competence of a contract not to revoke a will is confirmed by *Paterson* v *Paterson* (1893), although *McEleveen* v *McQuillan's Executrix* (1997) made clear that such a contract must be in writing.

Revocation may be express or implied. The testator may expressly revoke any earlier testamentary writing by inserting a "revocation clause" in his new will. A revocation clause makes clear that only this latest will represents the testator's completed testamentary intention, and earlier writings are revoked. Express revocation can also be carried out through destruction of a will. This may be straightforward physical destruction – such as burning the document in the fire – or symbolic destruction, where the will is scribbled out (as in *Cruickshank's Trustees* v *Glasgow Magistrates* (1887)), or cut into pieces (as in *Crosbie* v *Wilson* (1865)). The testator must have destroyed the document himself or instructed someone else to do so (as in *Cullen's Exr* v *Elphinstone* (1948)), in order for the destruction to operate as a valid revocation.

If the testator was known to have executed a will, but it cannot be found on his death, it is presumed that the will was destroyed by the testator. A person seeking to overturn this presumption must bring an action to "prove the tenor" of the will, establishing through evidence both the content of the will and the fact that it was not destroyed by the testator. In most cases, this will be very difficult to establish.

A will may also be revoked by implication. Where a will contains provisions which conflict with those in an earlier will by the same testator, it is presumed that the earlier will is revoked to the extent that it conflicts with the later document. Imagine, for example, that Olive executes a will in February, leaving her house to Padma and her jewellery to Rose. In December, she executes a second will, providing nothing other than that she leaves her house to Simon. The legacy of the house to Padma in the February document will be revoked by the conflicting legacy in favour of Simon in the December document. However, the legacy of the jewellery to Rose in the February document will continue to stand, since it creates no conflict with anything in the December document. If a later will disposes of the whole estate, the earlier deed must, logically, be revoked entirely, as in *Cadger* v *Ronald's Trustees* (1946).

Case law suggests that where a later will is itself revoked, a subsisting earlier deed will revive, although the position is not entirely clear. See further discussion in *Scott's JF* v *Johnston* (1971). In its 2009 Report at paras 6.31–6.36, the Scottish Law Commission proposes clarification of the law by recommending that a will which has been revoked should not revive unless the testator executes a document which expressly revives it.

One further mechanism by which a will may be revoked through implication is the *conditio si testator sine liberis decesserit*. This *conditio* operates where the testator has had a child subsequent to execution of the will. The law presumes that a testator would not deliberately omit to make provision for this child in the will. The effect of the *conditio* is to revoke all testamentary writings of the parent and render the estate intestate.

This does not happen automatically. Rather, the child born after the will was executed must decide whether they wish to invoke the *conditio*. The decision may not be straightforward. It should be recalled that a child in this position already has an entitlement to legal rights, which can be claimed from a testate estate. If there is a lot of money in the estate, the rules of intestacy may result in the child obtaining a larger amount of money than he would in legal rights alone. In such a case, invoking the *conditio* would be financially worthwhile for the child. However, if the estate is modest in size, pushing it into intestacy may result in prior rights eating up all the assets. In that case, the child will end up with nothing, and from a financial standpoint it would be better to take the modest legal rights claim available to him on the testate estate.

For example, imagine an estate consisting entirely of £30,000 in a bank account which has been left to the deceased's friend in the will. There is a surviving spouse, and one child, born after the will was executed. The child could claim legal rights over the testate estate. Since there is a surviving spouse, legitim will be calculated as to one-third of the moveable property, or £10,000. Alternatively, the child could invoke the *conditio*, rendering the estate intestate. The spouse would then be entitled to prior rights, as discussed in Chapter 5. There is not a house or any furniture for the spouse to claim, but the entire £30,000 would be paid over in respect of the money right. There would be nothing left in the estate to pay a legal rights claim, and the child would end up without an inheritance.

Where it can be shown that the failure of the testator to make a new will after the child was born was a deliberate choice on the testator's part, the presumption that the omission was a mistake will be overturned. Strong evidence will be required to prove that the choice was deliberate. The fact that a long period of time has elapsed between the birth of the child and the testator's death without a new will being made is not enough in itself to rebut the presumption, as demonstrated by *Milligan's JF* v *Milligan* (1910), in which 10 years had passed between the child's birth and the testator's death. There must be clear evidence of a positive intention on the part of the testator to exclude the child, as in *Stuart-Gordon* v *Stuart-Gordon* (1899). The testator was in ill health, and had executed her will around the time the child was born. Evidence showed that she knew the child would be well provided for by other sources. The court found that this combination of factors was sufficient to overturn the presumption, meaning that the *conditio* could not be invoked. The recent decision in *Greenan* v *Courtney* (2007) clarified that parole evidence of the testator's intention to exclude the child (in other words, evidence from other people of what the testator said, as opposed to something written by the testator himself) will not be sufficient to overturn the presumption.

In its 1990 Report at paras 4.46–4.49, the Scottish Law Commission noted that legal doctrines equivalent to the *conditio si testator* that once existed in other jurisdictions have generally been abolished, and considered that, in present-day Scotland, invoking the *conditio* may produce results far removed from what the testator would have wanted. It recommended abolition of the *conditio*. This recommendation was repeated in the 2009 Report at paras 6.18–6.21.

Essential Facts

- A valid will requires the testator to have had capacity and intention to test, and to have met the statutory formalities of writing.
- A testator will have capacity if aged 12 or over and mentally capable of understanding the effect of making a will.

- The validity of the will can be challenged if the testator's testamentary intentions were not freely expressed as a result of pressure put on him by someone else. The two grounds of challenge are facility and circumvention (where a vulnerable testator is deceived or misled by the other party) and undue influence (where the other party takes advantage of the trust placed in him by the testator).
- To be valid, the will must also comply with the Requirements of Writing (Scotland) Act 1995, meaning that it must be written down, signed on every page and subscribed by the testator.
- To be probative (self-proving), the testator's signature on the will must be witnessed. Where a will is probative, any person challenging the validity of that will has the responsibility of proving it to be invalid.
- A will may be revoked where the testator again has capacity and intention to do so.
- Express revocation takes place where the testator physically destroys the will, or sets out in writing that the will should be revoked.
- Implied revocation occurs where the testator writes a later will which conflicts with an earlier version, or where the *conditio si testator* is invoked by a child born after the will was executed.

Essential Cases

MacGilvary v Gilmartin (1986): in the days immediately following her husband's death, Mrs MacGilvary was taken to a solicitor by her daughter, Mrs Gilmartin, where she signed over rights in her house to her daughter. Mrs MacGilvary later argued that she was in an extreme state of grief and did not know what she was doing at the time. She wished to have the agreement set aside on the basis of facility and circumvention. The court accepted that the grief was enough to demonstrate facility on the testator's part, and also that she had suffered a loss in signing over her house. Although there was no specific evidence of circumvention, the high degree of both facility and loss allowed the court to infer that circumvention must have been present, and the agreement was set aside.

Gray v Binny (1879): the pursuer was in line to receive a substantial inheritance. The defender, his mother and her solicitor, with whom she was close, convinced the son to sign away his rights to the inheritance for far less than it was worth in order that the mother could pay off her debts. Evidence suggested that the son was not familiar with the business world and placed complete trust in his mother. Undue influence was held to exist, since the mother had taken advantage of the trust placed in her by her son in order to gain a benefit.

Nicol's Legal Representative v Nicol (2012): in a case brought by the legal representative of the deceased's daughter, evidence from a handwriting expert was used to prove that the deceased's purported will was in fact a forgery fabricated by the deceased's mother. In addition to reducing the will, the court interdicted the mother from confirming as executor to the deceased's estate.

7 LEGACIES

Since the purpose of a testamentary writing is primarily to set out how the testator wishes his assets to be distributed on his death, the major part of most testamentary writings will comprise legacies. A legacy is a provision stating who should receive part of the testator's property. The subject of a legacy is the property which has been bequeathed. The object of a legacy is the beneficiary of the bequest, also known as the legatee.

CATEGORIES OF LEGACY

Legacies are often categorised by subject. The four key types of legacy are as follows:

- A *specific legacy* is a bequest of a particular piece of property, such as a house or an item of jewellery. The subject must be clearly identified in the will and may be singular or plural, so a bequest of a collection of stamps would be a specific legacy in the same way as a bequest of a single Penny Black. If the subject has been destroyed or disposed of by the testator *inter vivos*, the legacy is not payable, and the beneficiary has no right to anything else in its place. In the example will at the end of this chapter, the legacy of the Fender Telecaster guitar is specific, with the description distinguishing it clearly from other guitars which may form part of the testator's estate. The legacy of shares in Apple Records Plc is also specific.

- A *demonstrative legacy* is a sub-category of a specific legacy, where the property bequeathed is a specific item from a specific named source. The most common example is a legacy of an amount of money to be paid from a particular bank account.

- A *general legacy* is a bequest of generic property which cannot be distinguished from other property of the same class. The most common example is a legacy of an amount of money with no specification as to the source from which the money should be paid. In the example will, the legacy of £300 is general.

- The subject of a *residual legacy* is the residue of the estate, meaning everything left in the estate after debts, legal rights claims and other legacies have been paid. It is not uncommon for the residue to represent the bulk of the estate, after small legacies have been left to individuals as tokens. The residual legacy is at cl Seven of the example will. Where a legacy in one of the other categories fails for any reason, the subject of that legacy will fall into the residue. Similarly, where a surviving spouse or child elects to take legal rights rather than the provision made for them in the will, the subjects of the legacy or legacies from which they would have benefited fall into the residue. If the residual legacy fails, the residue of the estate will become intestate and be distributed based on the rules of intestate succession, as discussed in Chapter 5.

A legacy may be *conditional*. The testator can provide that the legacy should pass to the beneficiary only if a certain condition is fulfilled (known as a suspensive condition). It is common, for example, for a testator to provide that a beneficiary should take a legacy "only if he survives me for fourteen days or more". Alternatively, the testator may provide that a legacy should pass to a beneficiary *unless* a certain condition is fulfilled (known as a resolutive condition). For example, it may be provided that a beneficiary should take a legacy "unless he is no longer in full time education at the time of my death". The law places certain limits on the types of condition a testator may impose, as discussed in Chapter 8.

Difficulties can arise in determining whether a direction in the will is a condition or a trust purpose. In *Dunbar* v *Scott's Trustees* (1872), the testator had left £2,000 to A if he had not purchased him a commission in the army at the time of his death. Was this a condition – that the money had not to pass unless a commission had not been purchased – or a trust purpose to the effect that the money, once inherited, was to be used to buy a commission? If the latter, the legacy would have failed for impossibility, since by that time it was no longer possible to purchase commissions in the army. The court construed it as a condition, and the money was paid.

A legacy may be described as *precatory* if it does not represent a completed testamentary intention on the part of the testator, but is merely a wish as to what might happen to the property in future. For a legacy to be precatory in its entirety is unusual. It is most likely that a valid legacy will contain precatory elements. For example, in *Milne* v *Smith* (1982) the testator left shares in two businesses to his son "it being my wish that both these businesses should be combined by my son and my brother". The legacy of the shares was valid, but the testator could not compel his son to enter into a partnership with his brother. That aspect of the bequest was merely precatory.

Legacies will usually involve transfer of ownership from the deceased's estate to the legatee. However, it is possible for the testator to make periodical provision for the beneficiary through the alternative mechanisms of *annuity* and *liferent*.

An annuity is the right to an annual payment from a specified source for a specified period of time. For example, Terry may include provision in his will that Una is to receive an annuity of 25 per cent of the income from Terry's premium bonds for 10 years after Terry's death, or until she remarries.

A liferent is a real right to the use and fruits of property for the duration of the holder's lifetime. If the property subject to the liferent is a house, the liferenter is entitled to occupy the house until death. If the property is, for example, a large sum of money in a savings account, the liferenter would be entitled to the interest earned on the money. If the property is shares in a company, the liferenter would be entitled to the dividends paid on the shares every year. What the liferenter does not have is ownership of the property (referred to in this context as the "fee"), which will be held by another person (the "fiar"). Accordingly, the liferenter cannot sell or destroy the property. Unlike the duration of an annuity, the duration of a liferent cannot be fixed by the testator. As the name suggests, liferent lasts for the lifetime of the holder. On the death of the liferenter, the fiar obtains the fee absolute – ownership, in the regular sense of the term.

Both an annuity and a liferent can be assigned by their holders to third parties. The exception to this rule is where the liferent is categorised as an alimentary liferent, designed to provide financially for the maintenance of a named person, usually a child of the testator.

ADEMPTION

Ademption means cancellation. If the subject of a legacy does not form part of the testator's estate on death, it is assumed that he disposed of it deliberately. Disposal implies that the testator did not have or no longer had the intention to bequeath the property and, in the absence of the necessary intention, that aspect of the will is considered to have been revoked.

A misdescription of the subject will not result in ademption. For example, if the Fender Telecaster guitar mentioned in the example will was in fact a Fender Stratocaster, and the testator did not own any other guitars, it is likely that the legacy would be interpreted as a bequest of the Stratocaster (*Door* v *Geary* (1749)). If, however, the testator did not own any guitars, the legacy would adeem.

Whether the subject of the legacy is part of the estate may not always be a straightforward question. The test to be applied is whether the substance of the bequest remains unchanged (*Stanley* v *Potter* (1789)). The case law on this point is not easy to reconcile. *Macfarlane's Trustees* v *Macfarlane*

(1910) found that where shares in a company were converted into stock in the same company, the essence of the property had not changed and so the legacy of the shares had not adeemed. However, in *Ballantyne's Trustees* v *Ballantyne's Trustees* (1941), it was held that a legacy of money in a particular bank account adeemed where the money had been transferred into a different bank account.

Where heritable property is in the process of transfer from the testator to a third party, a legacy of that heritage will not adeem if the transfer is incomplete at the time of the testator's death. However, the beneficiary will inherit the property subject to the conditions placed on the testator's ownership of it at the time of his death (*McArthur's Executors* v *Guild* (1908)). For example, the subject of the legacy may be a house, in respect of which the testator had concluded missives and delivered a disposition at the time of his death. At this stage of the transaction, the seller of a house is under strict legal obligations not to do anything that will prevent the buyer from obtaining ownership of the house through registration of the title. The legacy of the house will vest in the beneficiary, but it is subject to the same obligations that bound the seller-testator, meaning that the beneficiary cannot prevent the buyer from completing the sale transaction and acquiring ownership.

A testamentary writing will sometimes include an "anti-ademption" clause which will allow the testator some freedom to continue to deal with his property during his lifetime without negating the provisions of the will. An example would be a legacy of "my house at 12 Greenleaf Lane or such other heritable property as may be in my possession at the date of my death". If the testator were to sell the house at Greenleaf Lane and buy another property during his lifetime, the bequest would not adeem. Rather, the subject of the legacy would become the testator's new house.

Where the subject of the legacy is property which the testator did not own either at the time of execution of the will or on his death, the bequest may be interpreted as a *legacy rei alienae*. A legacy of this type is understood to be an instruction from the testator to acquire the property bequeathed for the beneficiary. For this doctrine to come into play, the testator must have been aware that he did not own the property at the time of making the bequest, and the subject must be clearly ascertainable, following *Macfarlane's Trustees* v *Macfarlane* (1910). For example, a bequest of 2,000 shares in Big Plc may be a legacy *rei alienae* if the testator was aware that he did not own any such shares. However, a bequest of "half my shares in Big Plc" cannot be a legacy *rei alienae* since it is impossible to ascertain how many shares the testator intended to bequeath.

ABATEMENT

Abatement means reduction. It may be the case that the property in the estate, after payment of debts and legal rights, is insufficient to pay all the legacies in full. In that case, each legacy will abate. Abatement occurs in a specific order, with residual legacies abating first, followed by general legacies, demonstrative legacies and then specific legacies. In other words, specific legacies are paid in full first. Demonstrative legacies are then paid in full, provided that there is sufficient in the specified source of the subject of the legacy for this to be done. General legacies are then paid in full. If there is anything left in the estate following payment of the general legacies, it will go to the residuary legatee(s).

Where there is more than one legacy within each of the categories, each will abate proportionately with the other legacies in that category. For example, if Victor has been left £100 and Wendy has been left £200 but only £150 remains in the estate, Victor will receive £50 and Wendy will receive £100. This cannot apply to specific legacies.

The order of abatement can be altered by specific provision in the will.

THE OBJECT OF A LEGACY

The object of a legacy is the person to whom the legacy has been left, also known as the legatee or the beneficiary.

The object of a legacy should be clearly identified. Minor errors, such as a spelling mistake, in the identification of a beneficiary can be ignored so long as it is otherwise clear who was intended to receive the bequest. If there is doubt over the correct beneficiary, other information within the will may be used to resolve the uncertainty. In *Macfarlane's Trustees* v *Henderson* (1878), a legacy was left to "my late brother James's son". The testator had a late brother James, who had a daughter, and also a surviving brother David, who had a son. The court considered it more likely that the testator would have made a mistake with the gender of his niece than with the name of his brother. Where there is nothing in the will which helps to resolve the problem, extrinsic evidence may be permitted. In *Keiller* v *Thomson's Trustees* (1824), the legacy was left to "Janet Keiller or Williamson". Was the legacy intended for Agnes Keiller/Wedderspoon or Janet Keiller/Whitton? Evidence of earlier testamentary writings was admitted, in which Agnes Wedderspoon had frequently been the object of a similar legacy. The court concluded that Williamson was an erroneous transcription of Wedderspoon here.

If it is not possible to determine the identity of the object, the legacy will be void. The subject of the legacy will fall into the residue or, if it is the residuary legatee who cannot be identified, the residue of the estate will fall into intestacy.

Legal presumptions exist in relation to certain objects. The first concerns any legatee identified as a husband, wife, spouse or civil partner of another party. If this legatee is named, and a term such as "spouse" is used simply as a description, that person will remain a valid legatee regardless of whether the relationship subsists by the time of the testator's death. For example, a legacy to "my wife Anne Smith" will pass to Anne Smith on the testator's death regardless of whether she continues to be his wife at that time (*Couper's JF v Valentine* (1976)). If the legatee is not named, the legacy will go to the person who holds the relevant status at the time of the testator's death. So a legacy to "my wife" will pass to whichever woman happens to be married to the testator at the point of his death. If he is not married at the time, the legacy will fail. In its 1990 Report at paras 4.34–4.45, the Scottish Law Commission recommended a simplification of this rule, so that divorce should have the effect of revoking any provisions in favour of a spouse named or otherwise, and the estate should be distributed as though that person had predeceased the testator. This recommendation was reiterated in its 2009 Report at paras 6.8–6.17.

Presumptions also apply where the objects of the legacy are a class of persons, usually those in a particular category of relationship such as the "siblings of X" or the "children of X". Unless the will provides otherwise, any person falling into the category at the time of the testator's death will be entitled to share in the legacy, even if they were not alive at the time the will was executed. The Succession (Scotland) Act 1964 clarifies at s 23(4) that legacies to children or issue are to include posthumous children, adopted children and children born outside of marriage. "Heirs" is defined to mean persons who would be entitled to succeed if the testator had died intestate. Where the testator makes a bequest to "children", it is usually only the immediate generation of descendants who are entitled to a share. Grandchildren or children of subsequent generations have no entitlement (unless the *conditio si institutus sine liberis decesserit* applies, as discussed in detail below). Where the bequest is made to "issue" rather than children, grandchildren and subsequent generations have an automatic entitlement to inherit the share their parent would have received, should their parent die before the testator. As an example, if a legacy is left to "my friend Michael Wood's children", and only grandchildren of Michael Wood were alive at the time of the testator's death, they would not be entitled to claim and the legacy would fail. However, if the legacy had instead been to "my friend

Michael Wood's issue", the grandchildren could take the inheritance in the place of their parents.

AVOIDING FAILURE OF A LEGATEE

A legatee must be alive in order to receive the legacy. If the legatee predeceases the testator, generally speaking, the legacy will fail. To avoid this result, the testator may include a "destination over" in the legacy, a mechanism by which an alternative beneficiary can be specified. If the testator has not done so expressly, in certain situations the law will imply a destination over.

In a legacy with a destination over, the primary legatee will be known as the *institute*. Depending on the mechanism used, the alternative beneficiary will be called the *conditional institute*, or the *substitute*.

- A *conditional institute* will inherit the legacy only if the institute predeceases the testator, or fails to survive another event specified by the testator in the will. If the institute survives the testator or meets the condition specified, she will take the bequest in full, and the conditional institute will have no entitlement. So, imagine that Alf leaves his car to Bella as the institute, whom failing to Cheryl as the conditional institute. If Bella dies before Alf, Cheryl will inherit the car. If Bella survives Alf, Bella will inherit the car, and Cheryl will receive nothing.

- A *substitute* will inherit the legacy after the death of the institute, even where the institute survives the testator. So, imagine that Alf has left his car to Bella as the institute, and Cheryl as the substitute. If Bella predeceases Alf, Cheryl will inherit the car as before. If Bella survives Alf, Bella will inherit the car – but Cheryl does not lose out entirely, as she would do as a conditional institute. Cheryl, as the substitute, will be entitled to inherit the car *on Bella's death*. That is the effect of substitution.

The right of the substitute is not, however, as strong as it may first appear. This is because the institute is not bound to adhere to the testator's intention that the legacy should go to the substitute on the institute's death. Instead, the institute has the power to make alternative provision for the property in question, either by transferring ownership of the property to another party during his lifetime, or by making a will in which the property is bequeathed to someone other than the substitute on the institute's death. This is known as *evacuating* the destination to the substitute. So, in the situation above where Cheryl is the substitute in respect of Bella's inheritance of Alf's car, Bella can evacuate the destination by selling the car during her lifetime, or by making a will in which she leaves the car to Donald.

A will may clearly specify whether an alternative legatee is intended to be a conditional institute or a substitute. However common forms of wording, such as a legacy "to A, whom failing B", do not indicate clearly which type of destination over is intended. Accordingly, presumptions apply in such cases based on the type of property which forms the legacy. If the legacy is of moveable property, conditional institution is presumed, subject to any evidence that the testator intended otherwise. If the subject of the legacy is heritage, then substitution will be presumed. Some useful discussion of the difficulties that can arise in applying these rules can be found in *Crumpton's JF* v *Barnardo's Homes* (1917). The Scottish Law Commission recommends that the rule should be altered so that conditional institution is presumed in every instance, as discussed in its 2009 Report at paras 6.61–6.65.

Where the testator wishes to includes an *express* destination over, the most common form of wording is "to A, whom failing B". The testator may also include a condition that the institute must survive him for a certain period of time, failing which B will inherit: "to A, on the condition that he survive me for 30 days, whom failing B".

Destinations over will be *implied* in line with two distinct doctrines: accretion; and the *conditio si institutus sine liberis decesserit*.

Accretion

The doctrine of *accretion* may operate where a legacy has been left to more than one person, for example "to A and B and C", or to a class of people, for example "to the children of A and B". Where one of the legatees dies before the testator, the law implies a destination over in favour of the other legatees in that group. So if the will reads "I leave £9,000 to A and B" this is understood to mean that A and B should share the money between them, but if one of them dies before the testator, then the survivor should inherit the whole £9,000. Another way of expressing this is to say that the predeceasing legatee's share in the legacy accresces to the surviving legatee(s).

Accretion can only operate where it is clear that the legacy was intended jointly, rather than severally, for the legatees. In other words, the testator intended that the property should be shared among however many people within the group of legatees survived him, rather than that each individual legatee should receive only a specific share of the property and nothing more. This may be clearly expressed in the will. If not, the law will assume that legacy is intended to be joint and therefore shared among whoever survives the testator *unless* words of severance are used. This rule was set out in *Paxton's Trustees* v *Cowie* (1886), where it was found that expression such as "equally among them", "in equal shares", "share and share alike" or anything with the same meaning would prevent the operation of accretion. So, where a legacy of £9,000 is left "to A and B equally between them" and A dies before the testator, B nevertheless receives only half of the legacy. The share of the legacy intended for A fails, and that property falls into the residue.

Words of severance do not, however, prevent the operation of accretion where the legacy is left to a class of persons, such as "my children equally among them" or "the issue of A and B in equal shares".

Conditio si institutus sine liberis decesserit

The *conditio* is described by Hiram as "the doctrine that even if no express provision is made for the contingency of a beneficiary's predecease, the testator would not have intended the legacy to lapse, but rather that his or his children should take the legacy instead" (para 9.22). In a limited number of situations, where the legatee is a close family member of the testator, the law assumes that the testator would have wanted the legatee's children to inherit in the legatee's place. The children become the conditional institute for the legatee and are prioritised over any other conditional institute, whether expressly created in the will or implied by the law. In a situation where the *conditio* applies, if the testator leaves a legacy to "A, whom failing B" and A dies before the testator, any surviving children of A have the right to inherit before B. Only if A dies childless before the death of the testator will B inherit the legacy.

The *conditio* applies to a very limited range of legatees. Where the institute is a child, grandchild or other direct descendant of the testator, the *conditio* will operate. Where the institute is a nephew or niece of the testator, the *conditio* will operate if the testator was *in loco parentis* of the legatee. *Bogie's Trustees* v *Christie* (1882) suggests that the fact that the testator left a legacy to his nieces and nephews in his will may be sufficient to meet the test of being *in loco parentis* in this context. It is not expected that the testator will have treated the niece or nephew as his own child during his lifetime. The Scottish Law Commission has recommended that the *conditio* should apply only to direct descendants of the testator (2009 Report, paras 6.22–6.30).

The operation of the *conditio si institutus* can be excluded by express provision to that effect in the will. It may also be excluded where the testator has made provision for the children of the institute elsewhere in his will, following *Greig* v *Malcolm* (1835). Whether the testator intended alternative provision to exclude the *conditio* will be a question of interpretation of the will as a whole.

Where more than one destination over exists in respect of a single legacy, the law sets out rules as to the order in which the beneficiaries are entitled to succeed. A conditional institute created by operation of the *conditio si institutus* will take in preference to a conditional institute created expressly in the will or by operation of the rules of accretion. If the *conditio* is not applicable, an institute created expressly will be preferred to an institute arising from accretion (*Devlin's Trustees* v *Breen* (1945)). The Scottish Law Commission effectively recommends that an express destination over should prevail over an implied destination over in all contexts (2009 Report, paras 6.22–6.30).

INTERPRETING LEGACIES

From the discussion above, it is clear that the effect of a provision in a will often depends on exactly how it is interpreted. Some general principles apply to assist in this interpretative process.

The aim of the court when interpreting testamentary writings will be to give effect to the testator's wishes based on what is said in the document. The court will favour an interpretation of particular words or clauses that avoid any part of the estate falling into intestacy.

In common with general principles of contractual interpretation, the will should be read as a whole document. Its meaning should be drawn from the words of the will itself without reference to extrinsic evidence, which is excluded by s 8 of the Law Reform (Miscellaneous Provisions) (Scotland) Act 1985. Extrinsic evidence may, however, be permitted where it is impossible to determine the meaning of the words without it. An example is the case of *Nasmyth's Trustees* v *National Society for the Prevention of Cruelty to Children* (1914). The testator had left a legacy to "the National Society for the Prevention of Cruelty to Children", which was claimed by both the London-based charity with that name and the equivalent Scottish organisation called the Scottish Society for the Prevention of Cruelty to Children. Extrinsic evidence was led to show that the testator, who was Scottish and whose estate was held entirely in Scotland, was not aware of the existence of the London-based charity. Nevertheless, the bequest was interpreted in favour of the English charity as being the one expressly named in the testament.

Essential Facts

- Wills are made up of legacies.
- The subject of a legacy is the property bequeathed. Legacies can be categorised by subject as specific, demonstrative, general or residual legacies.
- If the legacy cannot be paid because the property is not or no longer part of the testator's estate, it will adeem (be cancelled).
- If there is not enough in the estate to pay all the legacies in full, the legacies will abate (be reduced) in a particular order.
- The object of a legacy is the person to whom the legacy was left.
- The testator can create an alternative beneficiary to take the legacy if the original object dies. The alternative beneficiary may be a conditional institute, who will inherit if the original beneficiary dies before the testator; or a substitute, who will inherit *from* the original beneficiary after he dies.
- Destinations over can also be created by implication through the doctrine of accretion where the legacy is left to a group of people, or through the *conditio si institutus sine liberis decesserit* where the original legatee was a close family member of the testator and has been survived by children.
- General rules of interpretation of contract will apply to wills. The cardinal rule is that the will should be read in a way that gives effect to the testator's intentions.

Essential Cases

Macfarlane's Trustees v Macfarlane (1910): the deceased had owned shares in a company, and made a will leaving the shares to his mother and sisters. A few months before his death, the deceased became incapable of managing his own affairs, and a *curator bonis* was appointed to look after them. The *curator* sold the shares. Did the legacy therefore adeem? The court considered that action taken by a curator could not impact on the deceased's testamentary provision unless it was a necessary and unavoidable act on the *curator's* part. The shares had been sold in this case simply because the *curator* considered it prudent to do so. Accordingly, the legacy did not adeem, and the beneficiaries were entitled to receive the value of the shares from the estate.

Couper's JF v Valentine (1976): Roy Couper made a will in which his entire estate was left to "my wife, Mrs Dorothy Couper". He later divorced his wife for desertion. Several months after the divorce was granted, he died, without having made any change to his will. Was Dorothy Couper entitled to inherit the estate now that she was no longer his wife? The court did not consider the words of the will to imply that it was a condition of the inheritance that the beneficiary remain the testator's wife. The language was simply descriptive. Accordingly, the divorce had no effect on the legacy and the beneficiary was entitled to inherit the estate.

Crumpton's JF v Barnardo's Homes (1917): the testatrix had left a legacy to her nephew "and her heirs, executors and administrators absolutely", qualified by adding "in case my nephew shall die without issue" the legacy should be divided among certain charities, including Barnardo's Homes. The nephew survived his aunt but later died intestate and without children. The defender argued that it should now be entitled to a share in the legacy as substitute of the nephew. The court held that the qualification to the legacy was only entitled to take effect if the nephew had died without issue prior to the death of the testatrix. In other words, the destination over had the effect of making the charities conditional institutes rather than substitutes. Since the nephew had survived the testator, the defender accordingly had no right to inherit.

EXAMPLE WILL

This is one possible example of how a formally valid will could be written. Commentary on the will, which would not form part of the document, is written in italicised font within square brackets [*like this*].

LAST WILL AND TESTAMENT

I, JOHN WINSTON LENNON residing at One University Square, Hillhead, Glasgow, G12 3AB in order to settle the succession to my estate after my death provide as follows:

(ONE) I REVOKE all prior Wills and Testamentary Writings; [*This is known as a "revocation clause".*]

(TWO) I APPOINT LAW AND SONS, a Company incorporated under the Companies Act 1985 and having its Registered Office at

THREE UNIVERSITY STREET, GLASGOW to be my Executors; [*The testator has nominated a law firm to act as his executor. The final clause of the will sets out the powers the executor will be entitled to exercise.*]

(THREE) I LEAVE the sum of THREE HUNDRED POUNDS (£300) STERLING to my son, JULIAN LENNON of FOUR WILLOW CRESCENT, STIRLING. [*This is a general legacy.*]

(FOUR) I LEAVE my Fender Telecaster electric guitar to PAUL McCARTNEY of FIFTEEN OAK LANE, PERTH, whom failing to GEORGE HARRISON of TWENTY BIRCH AVENUE, ELGIN. [*This is a specific legacy. Paul McCartney is the institute and George Harrison is the alternative beneficiary. From the wording of the legacy, it is not clear whether George is intended to be a conditional institute or a substitute. Since the legacy is of moveable property, conditional institution will be presumed.*]

(FIVE) I LEAVE one half of my shares in APPLE RECORDS PLC to GEORGE HARRISON of TWENTY BIRCH AVENUE, ELGIN and RICHARD STARKEY of EIGHT PINE STREET, OBAN equally between them. [*This is a specific legacy. The words of severance – "equally between them" – prevent accretion from operating in respect of the legacy. This means that if George predeceases the testator, his half of the legacy will not go to Richard. Instead, it will fall into the residue.*]

(SIX) I LEAVE the sum of FIVE HUNDRED POUNDS (£500) STERLING to GREENPEACE, REGISTERED CHARITY NUMBER SC12345.

(SEVEN) I LEAVE the residue of my estate to my son SEAN LENNON residing at THREE ELM GARDENS, HILLHEAD, GLASGOW. In the event of the said SEAN LENNON failing to survive me I leave said residue to YOKO ONO residing at THIRTEEN POPLAR CRESCENT, HILLHEAD, GLASGOW. [*Sean is the residuary legatee. It is clear from the wording of the legacy that Yoko is intended to be a conditional institute, not a substitute.*]

(LASTLY) My Executors shall have the fullest powers of retention, realisation, investment, appropriation, transfer of property without realisation, and management of my estate as if they were absolute beneficial owners; and they shall have power to resign office and to appoint solicitors or agents in any other capacity from among their own number and to allow him or them the remuneration to which he, she or they would ordinarily be entitled: IN WITNESS WHEREOF these presents consisting of this and the one preceding page are executed as follows:

THEY ARE SUBSCRIBED BY ME, the said
JOHN WINSTON LENNON
at THREE UNIVERSITY STREET, GLASGOW
on the THIRD
day of MAY
in the year TWO THOUSAND AND THIRTEEN subscribing by my usual signature before this witness, namely: [*The words from IN WITNESS WHEREOF to here make up the testing clause, narrating the circumstances of the subscription and witnessing of the will.*]

J Lennon
[*Standard method of signature.*]

Witness: *Brian Epstein*
Brian Epstein
23 Main Street
Edinburgh
EH1 2AB
Salesman [*The occupation of the witness is usually stated.*]

8 RESTRAINTS ON TESTAMENTARY FREEDOM

The law places certain limitations on the extent of the testator's power to dispose of his property on his death. These legal restraints on freedom to test can be grouped into two main categories. In the first place, the law invalidates testamentary provisions deemed contrary to public policy, usually because they direct that the testator's money be used in a way that offers no benefit for individual people or the public in general. Second, the law prevents a testator from exercising too much control from "beyond the grave" by placing overly restrictive conditions on the object and the subject of the legacy.

PUBLIC POLICY

A legacy considered contrary to public policy will be invalid. The examples in the case law of legacies which have been struck out on this basis concern testators who are overly concerned with memorialising themselves after death, to the benefit of no-one.

The two best examples of legacies contrary to public policy are found in the cases of *McCaig v University of Glasgow* (1907) and *McCaig's Trustees v Kirk Session of United Free Church of Lismore* (1915). The testators in these two cases were siblings. In the first case, McCaig had directed that the income from his estate should be used in perpetuity to build towers and statues of himself and his family on his estate, justifying the expenditure on the ground that it was designed to provide inspiration and encouragement to Scottish artists. His sister challenged the will on the basis that it would disinherit the testator's family without a creating a benefit for anyone else. The court made clear that testamentary provision for a memorial or burial place of a regular scale were acceptable, but where the whole income of a large estate was dedicated to objects of "no utility", this would be unlawful, and the will was accordingly declared invalid.

The second case concerned the sister's will. Somewhat bizarrely, despite her successful challenge in the first case, the sister made provision in her own will for memorials after her death, similar to those her brother had attempted to create. The court again found the will invalid, stating that although a person can do what she likes with her money during her lifetime, this was not the case after death. The law would not support the useless waste of assets.

Several similar examples exist. In *Aitken's Trustees v Aitken* (1927), the testator was the last of a family who had been connected with Musselburgh for several centuries. He directed that part of Musselburgh High Street be demolished so that a massive statute in bronze, featuring the testator mounted on a horse, could be erected on the site. The court held that a bequest would be invalid if it conferred neither a patrimonial benefit on any person nor a benefit upon the public. The bequest in this case failed the test and was struck out. In *Sutherland's Trustee* v *Verschoyle* (1968), the testatrix had directed that her art collection be made available to the public in perpetuity after her death, and left money to pay for the purchase of a building in which the collection would be displayed along with the employment of a caretaker to look after it all. Since her collection was "a heterogeneous conglomeration with no group of material sufficient to provide or illustrate any historical or educational theme such as might attract scholar, student or even the general public", the provision was struck out as being contrary to public policy.

A contrasting example demonstrates that memorials are not always excessive or wasteful. In *Campbell Smith's Trustees* v *Scott* (1944), a large sum of money bequeathed to build a monument to the Royal Scots army regiment was considered neither extravagant nor contrary to public policy. The court confirmed that provision for a memorial was not in itself contrary to public policy, but the nature, purpose and value of constructing the memorial would be the key to determining whether a particular provision of this type would be valid or not.

INVALID RESTRICTIONS

As discussed in Chapter 7, the testator may place certain conditions on the right of a beneficiary to inherit under the will. Where a condition attached to a legacy is illegal, immoral or impossible, the legacy will remain valid but the condition will be declared *pro non scripto*, meaning that the legacy will be distributed as though the condition had not existed.

A condition which places constraints on the legatee's freedom to marry, by prohibiting marriage in its entirety, to certain persons or categories of people, or by requiring marriage by a certain age or to certain persons or categories of people, will be invalid on the ground of public policy (*Barker* v *Watson's Trustees* (1919)). Similarly, a condition on where or with whom a person can live may be declared invalid, particularly if the condition purports to prohibit the beneficiary from living with someone to whom they are related (*Fraser* v *Rose* (1849); *Balfour's Trustees* v *Johnston* (1936)).

Statute also places limits on the extent to which a testator can control the destiny of his property after death. Restrictions on the free circulation of property are considered detrimental to the economy, among other problems.

Historically in Scotland, heritage forming the ancestral seat of a wealthy family would be handed down from first son to first son in perpetuity through the use of a legal device called an entail. The vestiges of this practice were abolished by the Entail Amendment Act 1841 which barred the creation of successive liferents. So, Deepa may leave a liferent of her house to Evan, but she cannot specify that, on Evan's death, a further liferent to Franco should be created. This prevents the testator from controlling the property for more than one generation after his death.

Statute also limits the amount of income that can be accumulated in a trust set up by the testator's will. For more information on this complex topic, see Hiram, *Succession*, paras 10.2–10.7.

Essential Facts

- The law places limits on the testator's freedom where a legacy is contrary to public policy, or where the testator is trying to exercise too much control over the property or the legatee from "beyond the grave".
- Legacies are likely to be considered contrary to public policy if they do not confer any benefit on a person or on the public in general.
- Where a condition attached to a legacy is immoral, illegal, impossible or seeks to control who the legatee can marry or live with, the condition will be invalid, and the legacy will be distributed as though the condition did not exist.
- The testator cannot control what happens to his property for more than one generation after his death. Provisions contrary to this, such as provision for successive liferents, will be struck out.

Essential Cases

McCaig v University of Glasgow (1907) and McCaig's Trustees v Kirk Session of United Free Church of Lismore (1915): the testators in these two cases were brother and sister. Each had left a will with instructions that the income generated by their estates should be used to build monuments to them and their family on their land forever. Both wills were declared invalid by the court on the basis that memorials of this size and expense were a waste of assets, serving no public function, and so were contrary to public policy.

Campbell Smith's Trustees v Scott (1944): provisions in a will for a large monument to be constructed in commemoration of the Royal Scots army regiment was not contrary to public policy bearing in mind the size of the estate and the purpose of the monument.

9 WILL SUBSTITUTES

The testator may be able to make provision for the distribution of his property after death without writing a will. Other forms of testamentary device are commonly employed in Scotland and, particularly where the estate is relatively modest, it may be more straightforward to make provision in this way. Following s 36(2) of the Succession (Scotland) Act 1964, property effectively disposed of by means of a will substitute does not form part of the estate on death, since it does not require to vest in the executors. Accordingly, this property is not available to satisfy prior or legal rights claims.

The main forms of will substitute are special destination (including survivorship destination), nomination (including in respect of proceeds of a life insurance policy) and *mortis causa* donation.

SPECIAL DESTINATION

A special destination is a clause in the deed of title to property which sets out who should obtain ownership of the property on the death of the current owner. The word "special" denotes that the destination relates to this particular piece of property only. Special destinations are most commonly employed in relation to heritage, since they require a written deed of title to be used, and rights in heritage in Scotland must always be constituted in writing. A special destination in relation to moveable property is competent, but the existence of deeds of title for moveables is much less common. Special destinations are, however, sometimes seen in shares and insurance policies.

A survivorship destination is one form of special destination. It is used in respect of property owned in common between two or more people, each of whom wishes on their death for their share in the property to transfer to the co-owners. A husband and wife who own a house together may hold title as "Gail and Henry and the survivor of them". If Gail dies before Henry, her share in the house will automatically pass into his ownership, meaning that he will own the whole house. If Henry dies first, Gail will become the owner.

The fact that a title includes a survivorship destination does not prevent the parties from dealing with their share in the property during their lifetime, by selling it or donating it to another party, for example. The survivorship destination does not give a co-owner the right to veto a transaction.

The survivorship destination can also be evacuated (made ineffective) on death, if the party who dies first has made alternative testamentary provision for their share of the house. Evacuating a survivorship destination in this way is subject to fairly stringent requirements under s 30 of the Succession (Scotland) Act 1964. The party seeking to evacuate the destination in a testamentary writing must explicitly refer to the survivorship destination and state expressly that he wishes to evacuate it. A general statement at the start of a will that it revokes all prior testamentary writings will not be sufficient, since a special destination is not a testamentary writing. The party seeking to evacuate must also have power to do so. *Brown's Trustee v Brown* (1943) confirmed that a party who paid the full purchase price for a property owned in common between two people will always have power to evacuate. *Perrett's Trustees v Perrett* (1909) found that where both parties had contributed equally to the purchase price, an implied contract existed between them that neither would evacuate the survivorship destination.

Section 19 of the Family Law (Scotland) Act 2006 provides that divorce or annulment of a marriage, or dissolution of a civil partnership, revokes an unevacuated survivorship destination by deeming each party to have predeceased the other. This resolved an anomaly in the law which arose where spouses co-owned property, and on divorce one spouse transferred his half-share of the property to the other as part of the divorce settlement. If the spouse who now owned the whole house purported to make provision for it in her will without expressly evacuating the survivorship destination as required by s 30 of the 1964 Act, the destination would remain in effect on his death and the whole house would be transferred to her former spouse.

Although property subject to a survivorship destination does not form part of the estate, it is nevertheless available for satisfaction of the rights of creditors, which must be paid before any other claims on the estate. This rule, confirmed in *Fleming's Trustees v Fleming* (2000), is explained by the fact that the substitute (in this case, the survivor) cannot take a greater right than that held by the institute. Since the deceased's ownership was subject to the rights of the creditor, the survivor's ownership must be similarly encumbered.

NOMINATION

This is a less common form of will substitute. Statute provides that a holder of an account with certain financial institutions, principally friendly societies, can nominate a person to receive any funds remaining in the account on his death. The nomination takes effect like a special destination, with funds vesting immediately in the nominee rather than in the executor. Revocation of the nomination is possible only by following the procedure set out in statute: as with special destinations, a clause in a will revoking prior testamentary writings will not affect a nomination. The current statutory provisions allowing for disposal of property on death by nomination are listed in Sch 2 to the Administration of Estates (Small Payments) Act 1965. The 1965 Act also limits the amount of money in one account capable of disposal by nomination to £5,000.

The proceeds of a life insurance policy may pass to a nominated beneficiary in much the same way, and will accordingly not form part of the deceased's estate. If no beneficiary has been named, and the proceeds are to be paid to the deceased's executors, they will form part of the estate in the usual way. A third alternative is that the policy may have been taken by the deceased in trust for their spouse or children. Such an arrangement will be regulated by the Married Women's Policies of Assurance (Scotland) Act 1880, which has been amended to apply to husbands and civil partners. If the policy specifies that it is being held in trust for the spouse and/or children, the proceeds will again pass directly to the beneficiary without vesting in the executors.

MORTIS CAUSA DONATION

The final form of will substitute is the *mortis causa* donation. This describes the situation where a testator, during their lifetime, transfers ownership of property to another person, subject to a condition that the testator may revoke the transfer at any point prior to their death. The donee is therefore holding the gift on behalf of the testator until their death. On the face of it, this may look exactly like a straightforward, unconditional gift and it can be difficult to prove that the testator had an alternative intention without written evidence to that effect. (The Scottish Law Commission recommends the introduction of a presumption that a gift is presumed to be an outright donation unless the donor clearly stipulates otherwise – 2009 Report, paras 7.38–7.41.) Since property forming the subject of a *mortis causa* donation remains subject to revocation by the testator until death, it forms part of the estate and is available for satisfaction of debts. However, *Morris* v *Riddick* (1867) confirms that the donee's right is good against the executor, meaning that the gift cannot be used to pay any legacies under the will.

Essential Facts

- A party can make provision for what should happen to his property on death without a will by using a different legal device. The most common will substitutes are special destination, nomination and *mortis causa* donation.
- A special destination is a clause in the title deed to a piece of property specifying who should inherit that property on the owner's death. Where property is owned in common by two or more people, a special destination providing for the deceased's share to be inherited by the other co-owners is known as a survivorship destination.
- Limited amounts of money held in accounts with particular types of non-mainstream financial institution can be left to another person by nomination. The proceeds of a life insurance policy can also be inherited in this way.
- A *mortis causa* donation is a transfer of ownership from one person to another subject to a condition that the donor can revoke the transfer at any point prior to his death. If he has not done so, on death the donee becomes the unconditional owner of the property.

Essential Cases

Perrett's Trustees v Perrett (1909): the deceased has made a will revoking all prior testamentary writings. Included in his estate was heritable property which the deceased had bought together with his wife. Each had contributed one-half of the purchase price, and the title was held by each of them and to the survivor of them. Had this special destination in favour of the deceased's wife been evacuated by the will? The court considered that since the property was heritable and both spouses had contributed one-half of the price, the destination was contractual in nature, with each spouse agreeing to take the chance of inheriting the other spouse's share. A contract cannot be altered by one of the parties acting unilaterally. Accordingly, it was not possible for the deceased's will to have evacuated the survivorship destination in favour of the deceased's wife.

Fleming's Trustees v Fleming (2000): a husband and wife owned a house between them and to the survivor of them. The husband had been sequestrated ("gone bankrupt") and subsequently died. Was his half-share of the house, which passed to his wife on his death by virtue of the survivorship destination, subject to the claims of his creditors? The court held that it was. His wife, as his substitute, could not hold a better right than the deceased had. His share in the house was subject to the claims of his creditors, and accordingly the creditors had the right to enforce those claims against his wife up to the value of his share in the property.

10 VESTING

Property vests in a person when they acquire an indefeasible right to it. Acquisition of this right can happen at an entirely separate time from the point at which ownership or possession of the property is acquired.

The concept of vesting plays a role at various stages in the succession process. The estate vests in the executor at the moment confirmation is granted. Legal rights to an intestate estate vest at the point of the intestate's death. The right of a legatee under a will vests at the moment of the testator's death, or at some later stage if that is provided for in the will.

WHAT IS A VESTED RIGHT?

A vested right to a piece of property is not the same as ownership. Rather, it is a personal right to have that property transferred or paid to the holder of the vested right in due course. In the succession context, the right is most often held by a legal rights claimant or a beneficiary against the executor of the estate.

Like other personal rights, a vested right can be assigned to another person or included within the holder's will. This can be important where a will provides that payment of a legacy is postponed until a certain time. For example, Imran's will might leave a legacy of £5,000 to Julie, not to be paid until Julie is 21, whom failing to Karl. Imran dies when Julie is 18. At this stage, the right to payment of the legacy vests in Julie, although that right cannot be exercised until she turns 21. Julie then dies at the age of 19. Since the right to the £5,000 is already vested in Julie, it is part of her estate on death. The right to the money will therefore pass on to Julie's heirs. It will *not* pass to Karl. Karl would only have taken the legacy if Julie had died *before* Imran. Since Julie survived Imran, the legacy had already vested in her.

WHEN DO RIGHTS IN SUCCESSION VEST?

Rights that arise on intestacy vest at the point of death. Rights arising under a will are more complicated, however, since the testator has the power to determine the time at which the legacy vests. The earliest point at which a right can vest is on the testator's death. The latest point is the date when payment of the legacy falls due.

The point at which vesting should occur may be clearly expressed in the will. However, ambiguity can arise as to the testator's intentions in this regard. The law has set out a series of rules which will operate to determine the testator's intentions where they are not clearly expressed. The general rules of interpretation of wills apply, meaning that the ultimate goal of the law here is to ascertain the testator's true intention. There is a presumption against an interpretation that will result in intestacy. In the absence of anything to suggest the contrary, it will be presumed that the legacy was intended to vest at the earliest possible date, in other words the date of the testator's death. If that interpretation is clearly excluded by the wording of the will, the next presumption will be that vesting was intended to be postponed until the date of payment. The wording of the will itself may overturn this presumption also, however.

VESTING OF CONDITIONAL LEGACIES

Legacies may sometimes be subject to conditions, as discussed in Chapter 7. For example, Imran might leave a legacy of £5,000 to Liam provided that he is still in full-time education. The requirement that Liam is still a student is a condition of his inheritance. If he fulfils (or "purifies" in the legal terminology) the condition, he will receive the legacy. If he does not, the legacy will pass to an alternative legatee, or fall into the residue. It is as though Imran had left the legacy to a person who does not exist. No person called Liam in full-time education existed at the point of Imran's death, and so the legacy would be treated as it would in any situation where the legatee had failed, as discussed in Chapter 7.

The effect of the condition attached to a legacy on vesting will depend on how it is expressed. The condition may relate simply to payment of the legacy, as with Julie's legacy of £5,000 not to be paid until she reached 21. In that case, the legacy will vest at the point of the testator's death as usual.

Alternatively, the condition may be a requirement of the inheritance itself, rather than simply a question of the timing of payment. The condition that Liam still be in full-time education is an example. In Liam's case, the condition was not fulfilled at the point of the testator's death, so the legacy did not vest.

Conditions may also relate to future events in the lives of legatees. A legacy may be left to Miriam provided that she reaches the age of 18. Unlike Julie's case, this is not simply a delay in payment. Miriam must reach the age of 18 or she has no right to the legacy. How does a future condition of this kind impact on vesting? The law draws a distinction between future events which will definitely happen, known as *dies certus*, and future events which may or may not ever happen, known as *dies incertus*. The most obvious example of a *dies certus* is death, since everyone will die at some point. Common examples of *dies incertus* include the marriage of a person, or a person attaining a particular age. Where the condition attached to the legacy is a *dies certus*, the legacy vests immediately at the point of death, since the future event will definitely happen. A *dies certus* condition is essentially just a delay in payment. However, where the condition is a *dies incertus*, the legacy cannot vest unless and until the uncertain event actually happens. Conditions of this kind are sometimes described as "suspensive conditions", since vesting is postponed unless and until the condition is purified.

An example may help to illustrate the difference. Imran may leave a legacy of £5,000 to Nick on his mother's death, and another legacy of £5,000 to Orla on the birth of her first child. Nick's mother is inevitably going to die at some point, so that legacy will vest in Nick at the point of Imran's death. However, Orla may or may not ever have children. The legacy to Orla cannot vest in her until the point at which her first child is born.

Why is it important whether the legacy has vested or not? Nick cannot obtain the money until his mother dies; Orla cannot obtain the money until she has a child. Whether or not the legacy has vested beforehand would seem to make no practical difference. In so far as it affects Nick and Orla directly, this is largely correct, although Nick may assign his vested right to someone else if he so chooses, for whatever that might be worth – an option not open to Orla. However, the question of vesting becomes most significant for Nick and Orla's heirs. If Nick dies before his mother does, he will not have been able to obtain the money left to him by Imran at any point during his lifetime. However, the right to the legacy had already vested in him. It therefore forms part of his estate, and will be inherited in turn by his heirs. Conversely, if Orla dies before she has had a child, no right to the money from Imran has ever vested in her, and her heirs will not be entitled to that legacy.

Ascertaining whether the testator intended to impose a suspensive condition or simply to suspend payment of the legacy is not always an easy task. A common form of wording may be "to Poppy on turning 40". Is this a suspensive condition, indicating that Poppy is to receive the legacy only if she reaches 40? Or is it intended that the legacy should vest on the testator's death, with payment suspended until Poppy's 40th birthday? The case law on interpretation of legacies of this type is complex and possibly conflicting. Detailed discussion can be found in the further reading listed at the end of this book.

One common situation in which there is a question as to whether a condition postpones vesting or simply postpones payment is where the legacy contains a survivorship clause.

Imagine that Imran leaves a legacy to his nieces Ruby, Rose and Rachel and the survivor of them, to be paid on their mother's death. What is the event beyond which the nieces must survive before the legacy will vest in them? Their mother's death is a *dies certus*, so, under the rules outlined above, vesting should occur at the point of Imran's death. In that case, it would seem to follow that the nieces need only survive until the moment of Imran's death, at which time the legacy will vest, with payment suspended until their mother dies. However, the law does not take this approach. In *Young v Robertson* (1862) the court set out the presumption that, as a general rule of construction, survivance should be taken to refer to the date of payment of a legacy.

DEFEASIBLE VESTING

In a limited number of situations, the law will allow a legacy to be subject to a resolutive condition. A resolutive condition is in some sense the opposite of a suspensive condition: it means that the legacy vests in the legatee *unless and until* the specific event occurs. The usual example is that a legacy will vest unless and until a named person has children, in which case the legacy should go to them instead.

The law in this area is again complex. However, in general, a resolutive condition can only be attached to a legacy in which payment has been suspended. The justification for this may be largely pragmatic: if the legacy vests and is paid immediately to the legatee, how can they be made to repay in the event that the resolutive condition is purified?

Most commonly a resolutive condition will be placed on a legacy of property which has been left to one party in liferent, and a second party in fee. A liferent is a real right in Scots law entitling the holder to make use of the property for the duration of their lifetime. The fee is ownership of that property subject to the liferent. Imran might leave his house to Sophie in liferent and Tom in fee. This would allow Sophie to live in Imran's house for the remainder of Sophie's life, although Tom will be the owner of it. In such a situation, Imran might apply a resolutive condition to the legacy to Tom, saying that he is to take in fee unless Sophie has children, in which case the children are to be preferred. At the point at which Imran dies, the liferent vests in Sophie and the fee vests in Tom. If Sophie has a child, the fee comes out of Tom's patrimony and vests instead in Sophie's child.

Essential Facts

- A vested right to a piece of property is a personal right to obtain ownership of that property. In the succession context, the right is usually held against the executor of the estate.
- Rights arising on intestacy will vest in the beneficiaries at the moment when the intestate dies.
- A testator may specify when rights arising under a will should vest. The earliest point at which vesting can occur is on the testator's death. The latest point is on the date when payment is due.
- A legacy subject to a *dies certus* condition, such as a death, will vest in the beneficiary immediately on the testator's death. A legacy subject to a *dies incertus* condition, such as a marriage, will not vest unless and until the condition is fulfilled.

GLOSSARY

beneficiary: A person receiving property under a testamentary writing or on intestacy.

codicil: An extra piece of writing added on to a will at a later date.

declarator: A type of court order which declares that a factual situation exists, for example declarator of marriage or declarator of death.

decree: The final decision by the judge in a court case.

estate: All the property someone owns. Includes intangible things such as rights and debts, as well as tangible assets and money.

executor: A person responsible for ingathering and distributing the deceased's estate. In this book, this term is gender neutral, although, historically, the term "executrix" has been used to refer to a female executor.

Exr/Exrx: Abbreviations of "Executor" and "Executrix" in case names.

intestate: Without a will.

issue: Children, grandchildren and any further generations of descendants.

judicial factor: Someone appointed by the court to take care of the affairs of another person who is no longer able to make decisions for himself, for example because of illness.

legacy: An item, an object or a sum of money left to a beneficiary in a will.

legatee: The recipient or beneficiary of a legacy.

next-of-kin: No formal legal meaning, but usually used to mean a person's spouse or civil partner and/or the nearest blood relative(s) based on the hierarchy of relations in the Succession (Scotland) Act 1964, s 2.

testament: Any deed that creates and gives effect to a person's intentions as to the disposal of his property after his death. Sometimes referred to as a "testamentary disposition".

testator: A person making a testamentary writing. In this book, this term is gender neutral, although, historically, the term "testatrix" has been used to refer to a female testator.

Tr/Trs: Abbreviations of "Trustee" and "Trustees" in case names.

will: The most common type of testamentary writing.

FURTHER READING

Introduction

Hiram, H, *Succession*, Chapter 2

Lee, N, *Revenue Law: Principles and Practice* (29th edn, 2011), Chapter 4

MacDonald, D R, *Succession*, Chapters 2–3 and 14–15

Paisley, R, "The succession rights of the unborn child" (2006) 10(1) Edin LR 29

Reid, K G C, De Waal, M J and Zimmermann, R (eds), *Exploring the Law of Succession* (2007)

Executors and the administration of the estate

Currie, J G, *Confirmation of Executors* (8th edn by E M Scobbie, 1995)

MacDonald, D R, *Succession*, Chapter 13

Meston, M C, *The Succession (Scotland) Act 1964* (5th edn, 2002), Chapter 8

Death and survivorship

Hiram, H, *Succession*, Chapter 1

MacDonald, D R, *Succession*, Chapter 1

Legal rights

Gardner, J C, *The Origin and Nature of the Legal Rights of Spouses and Children in the Scottish Law of Succession* (1928)

Hiram, H, *Succession*, Chapter 3

Hiram, H, "Reforming succession law: legal rights" (2008) 12 Edin LR 81

Meston, M C, *The Succession (Scotland) Act 1964* (5th edn, 2002), Chapter 5

Reid, D, "From the cradle to the grave: politics, families and inheritance law" (2008) 12 Edin LR 391

Reid, D, "Reform of the law of succession: inheritance rights of children" (2010) 14 Edin LR 318

Intestate succession

Burns, F, "Surviving spouses, surviving children and the reform of total intestacy law in England and Scotland: past, present and future" (2013) 33(1) *Legal Studies* 85

Hiram, H, *Succession*, Chapter 4

Kerrigan, J, "Section 29 of the Family Law (Scotland) Act 2006 – the case for reform?" 2008 SLT 175

Kerrigan, J, "Testamentary freedom revisited – further erosion?" 2012 SLT 29

MacDonald, D R, *Succession*, Chapter 4

McCarthy, F, "Rights in succession for cohabitants: *Savage* v *Purches*" (2009) 13(2) Edin LR 325

Meston, M C, *The Succession (Scotland) Act 1964* (5th edn, 2002), Chapters 4 and 6

Norrie, K McK, "Reforming Succession Law: Intestate Succession" (2008) 12(1) Edin LR 77

Reid, D, "From the cradle to the grave: politics, families and inheritance law" (2008) 12 Edin LR 391

Validity of testamentary writings

Hiram, H, *Succession*, Chapters 5 and 6

MacDonald, D R, *Succession*, Chapters 6 and 8

Legacies

Barr, A, Dalgleish, A and Stevens, H, *Drafting Wills in Scotland* (2nd edn, 2009), Chapters 3–6

Hiram, H, *Succession*, Chapters 8 and 9

MacDonald, D R, *Succession*, Chapter 10

MacDonald, D R, "Lapse of legacies" in E Cooke (ed), *Modern Studies in Property Law: Volume 1* (2001)

Restraints on testamentary freedom

Chalmers, J, "Testamentary conditions and public policy" in K G C Reid, M J De Waal and R Zimmermann (eds), *Exploring the Law of Succession* (2007)

Hiram, H, *Succession*, Chapter 10

MacDonald, D R, *Succession*, Chapter 9

Will substitutes

Hiram, H, *Succession*, paras 2.10–2.23

MacDonald, D R, *Succession*, Chapter 5

Vesting

Candlish Henderson, R, *The Principles of Vesting in the Law of Succession* (2nd edn, 1938)

MacDonald, D R, *Succession*, Chapter 11

INDEX